F~ Bill

GRACE UNDER PRESSURE:
What Gives Life To American Priests

**A STUDY OF EFFECTIVE PRIESTS
ORDAINED TEN TO THIRTY YEARS**

Funded by the Lilly Endowment, Inc.

James Walsh

John Mayer

James Castelli

Eugene Hemrick

Melvin Blanchette

Paul Theroux

Copies can be ordered from:
NCEA
Publication Sales
1077 30th Street, NW, Suite 100
Washington, DC 20007-3852
(202) 337-6232

Second Printing 1995

ISBN 1-55833-160-3

Contents

PART TWO: RELATED QUESTIONS

Introduction

Rev. James Walsh

Anyone who reads the newspaper knows that Catholic priests in the United States face historic challenges. Pressures abound! The priest shortage grows more severe with no end in sight, producing greater demands on fewer priests to minister to a growing number of people. The explosion of lay ministry produces more and new questions about the role of the priesthood. There are questions and deep feelings within the Church around the issue of who should be eligible for ordination. There are the expectations that the priest be an effective preacher, presider, teacher, theologian, canon lawyer, counselor, spiritual director, team and community builder, group facilitator, organizational developer, program planner, fund raiser, and financial manager. The scandals involving priest pedophilia cases that have come to light over the past decade have tarnished the priesthood's public image. It is no wonder, then, that there is considerable talk about the crisis in priests' morale.

And yet, there is no objective evidence that such a crisis actually exists. In fact, three recent studies show just the opposite:

- An NCEA study of priests ordained five to nine years, conducted in 1990, found that more than 80 percent would choose the priesthood again, about 90 percent said they were "very" or "pretty" happy, and four in five said that they encourage new vocations.

- A survey conducted by the Los Angeles Times in early 1994 found that 87 percent of priests said that they would renew their vows. While 59 percent of priests said the Church should ordain married priests, only 15 percent said they would marry if they could.
- A study conducted for the National Federation of Priests Councils in 1994 found that priests had the same level of emotional well-being as married men of the same age and income levels. Eighty-seven percent said they were very unlikely to leave the priesthood.

Why is priests' morale so high? In this study, funded by the Lilly Endowment, we sought to examine what contributes to the morale of priests. What is it that gives life to priests who are effective and respected in their ministry?

Roman Catholic priests have been the object of a number of intriguing sociological, demographic, and psychological studies. These studies have provided extremely useful data and insights into the habits of priests, their level of satisfaction with their ministry, and problem areas. Despite the number of studies conducted, however, there have been few, if any, anthropological studies of American Catholic priests. Sociological studies try to get at what people do (their observable behavior). Psychological studies try to get at what people think or feel (their internal, mental, or emotional behavior). An anthropological study provides a forum for people to tell the stories of their lives and then discerns from those stories the symbols and patterns which sustain people, give them life, keep them engaged and committed, provide meaning, and give them hope for the future. The purpose of this type of study regarding the priesthood would be to discover whether there are such symbols and patterns that are operative in the lives of successful Roman Catholic priests. Such a study uses participation, listening, and interpretative analysis.

The initial discussion of an anthropological study of the priesthood included: Rev. Gerald Brown, SS., currently president of the Conference of Major Superiors of Men; Rev. Melvin Blanchette, SS., director of personnel for the Society of St. Sulpice; Rev. Paul Theroux of the United States Catholic Conference Bishops' Committee on Priestly Formation; Rev. Eugene Hemrick, director of research for the National Conference of Catholic Bishops; and myself, the executive director of the seminary department of the National Catholic Educational Association. Hemrick's presence assured continuity with his previous studies on seminarians and priests: *Seminary Life and Visions of the Priesthood* (1987), *A Survey of Priests Ordained Five to Nine Years* (1991), *and Seminarians in the Nineties* (1993).

This core team decided to implement a study involving scientifically selected focus groups of priests from around the country. This methodology would provide priests an opportunity to talk about the priesthood. We wanted to learn what gives their lives meaning, what events have caused turning points in their life, what images and perspectives most influence them, what relationships sustain them, and what traditions best help them cope and stay alive in the priesthood, during these pressure-packed times.

Once the general methodology was agreed upon, the next step was to form the research team, which included:

Hemrick; Blanchette; Theroux; Dr. John Mayer, a psychologist who works for the Archdiocese of Chicago and had conducted clinical interviews with dozens of priests for another study; James Castelli, a writer with 25 years experience writing about Church issues; and myself.

The team met in February, 1994 to design the full study. In a day-long session, we agreed to conduct focus groups in the following four regions of the country at sites within a reasonable driving distance of the dioceses involved.

- Eastern Region: Archdiocese of Baltimore, Archdiocese of Washington, Diocese of Wilmington, Diocese of Arlington

- Midwestern Region: Archdiocese of Cincinnati, Archdiocese of Indianapolis, Archdiocese of Louisville, Diocese of Covington

- Southern Region: Archdiocese of New Orleans, Diocese of Baton Rouge, Diocese of Lafayette, Diocese of Biloxi

- Western Region: Archdiocese of San Francisco, Diocese of Oakland, Diocese of San Jose, Diocese of Sacramento

In each of these dioceses five leaders with an overview of the diocesan personnel were contacted: the bishop; the head of the priests' personnel board; the head of the office of continuing education of clergy; and two other directors in each diocese who were laymen or laywomen, for example, the director of religious education, the editor of the diocesan newspaper, the director of pastoral ministry, or the director of evangelization. The total of 80 diocesan leaders included 17 bishops, 31 priests, 6 religious women, 1 religious brother, 10 laywomen, and 15 laymen. These individuals were asked to name, as potential participants in the focus groups, five priests who met the following criteria:

- ordained 10 to 30 years
- diocesan or religious
- respected for priesthood by laity and priests
- enthusiastic and effective in life and ministry
- has a sense of his own identity as a priest

Responses would provide a possible pool of 25 names per diocese. In the selection process for the focus groups first preference ·vould be given to those priests who appeared on more than one leader's list. If no one appeared on more than one list, a random sampling of those listed once would be performed.

Sixty-five diocesan leaders responded naming a total of two hundred forty-seven (247) different priests. Thirty-six priests' names appeared on at least two lists, eliminating the need for a random sample of those who appeared on only one list. Some names appeared on three lists and one appeared on four. One priest named himself, but two other people named him as well.

As a result of the selection process nine priests from each region were invited to be participants in the focus groups. In the Eastern, Midwestern, and Southern regions nine priests accepted and participated, and in the Western region eight priests.

Here is a demographic rundown on the focus group participants:

Length of Time in the Priesthood: The average number of years in the priesthood was twenty-one. Ten years of priesthood was the fewest and thirty-one the most. The priests in the sample represented 717 years of ordained ministry.

Age: The average age was 47. Two priests were under 40, one 37 and one 39. Two were over 60, one 61 and one 62.

Parents: Only two priests had parents who were divorced. All of the priests were raised as Catholics.

Early Church Involvement: Thirty-one of the thirty-five priests had been altar boys; 25 were involved in some other form of Church service when they were young, e.g., choir, lector, catechist. Only one priest was not involved in any Church service prior to seminary.

Age First Thought About Priesthood: These priests had first thought about the priesthood, on average, at age 12. A few said they had thought about the priesthood at age four or five. The oldest had thought about becoming a priest at age 28 after having been a religious brother.

Ministries: At the time of the focus groups, twenty-three of the priests were pastors. Of those, sixteen priests were full-time pastors; seven had another job besides pastor. Two priests were associate pastors. Eight priests were full-time chancery officials, and two were in education. All had parish experience but two whose only background was in education. Twenty-five had been pastors and thirty-one had been associate pastors.

When we looked at the priests' past and present experience, we found that 28 different ministries were represented:

Pastor - 25
Associate Pastor - 31
Vocation Director - 8
High School Teacher - 8
Director of Continuing Education of Priests - 7
Vicar for Priests/Personnel Director - 6
Tribunal - 6
Campus Minister - 5
Chancellor - 4
Vicar General - 3
Hospital Chaplain - 3
Director of Worship - 3
Director of Youth Ministry - 3
Seminary Professor - 3
High School Principal - 2
Director of Family Life - 2
National Conference of Catholic Bishops' Staff - 2
Director of Pastoral Planning - 1
Director of Marriage Encounter - 1
Director of Renew - 1
Director of Missions - 1
Director of Evangelization - 1
Director of Hispanic Ministry - 1
Director of Campus Ministry - 1
Secretary to Bishop - 1

Rector of the Seminary - 1
President of a Catholic College - 1
Liaison with Charismatic Renewal - 1

A list of four questions developed by the research team was presented to each of the focus groups:

- *What gives life to your priesthood?*
- *How do you deal with the controversies facing the Church today?*
- *How do you see your role as a man in American society?*
- *What advice would you give to seminary personnel today?*

Each of the four focus groups lasted approximately three hours and thirty minutes. Dr. John Mayer conducted the groups and I served as moderator. Each session was recorded. Fifteen hours of audio tapes were transcribed so that each member of the research team had a text with which to work. After studying the transcripts, the team met for two full days to identify and discuss the themes and patterns which emerged.

This book is divided into two parts. The first part focuses on the many responses to the question, "What gives life to your priesthood?" At least ninety minutes of each focus group was spent discussing this question.

These responses were organized into 12 major categories. While the categories are distinguishable, they are interrelated. For example, it was found that successful, effective priests enjoy a wide variety of deep personal relationships with family, friends, other priests, religious sisters, couples, laymen and laywomen, and members of support groups. It was also found that on the professional level these priests draw life from the people they serve; their parishioners serve as models, ministers, and sources of inspiration. These are separate patterns, but they are clearly related.

In the same vein, their statements showed that these effective priests experience God's love for them, see Jesus as a model for their behavior, have deep spiritual lives, and have a strong sense of the mystery of God that underlies the life of the Church and their own personal lives and ministries. Again, these are distinguishable patterns, but they, too, are clearly related to one another.

The second half of the book addresses the priests' responses to the three remaining questions. The reader will notice that the answers to these questions replay some of the themes and patterns of life for these priests.

We promised the priests in our focus groups anonymity, so we have changed their names.

Finally, the research team tried in vain to find one phrase that all agreed would completely capture the essence of the priests in this study. Accordingly, then, several terms are used throughout this book because they all capture some element of these priests. Sometimes they are "effective priests," other times "respected priests." Each term applies equally.

We were not surprised by the fact that the morale of the priests in our focus groups was so high. After all, others had identified them as "enthusiastic and effective in life and ministry." But we were a bit taken aback at the richness of the response. Some of the men knew one another, others met for the first time. There was a level of trust that became apparent as soon as the first priest in each group began to witness. The listening to each story by everyone in the room was intense. At lunch after the sessions a number of the priests talked about how inspiring and encouraging that exchange had been for them. One priest remarked, "I feel like I've just been on retreat!"

I had a sense of being on sacred ground. It was a gift to be enlightened and inspired by the stories of how God moved these good men and gave them life. They witnessed to the pressures involved in the priesthood today. They also witnessed to the Good News that, underlying the pressures, the activities, the relationships, and the expectations, is the presence and activity of a loving God. They witnessed to the grace in all of that, under all of that!

Part One

What Gives Life to Your Priesthood?

In the responses to this question twelve general categories or patterns emerged.

1. Risk Taking and Change

Living on the razor's edge. Pushing back the horizon. Jumping off of cliffs. Being on the cutting edge. Getting the juices going. Finding more hills to climb. Being a change agent. Being like a fireman who gets an adrenaline or endorphin rush when the fire bell rings.

That's the way priests describe their lives in the priesthood. In earlier research, Dr. John Mayer found that the personalities of successful priests have much in common with the personalities of fighter pilots, i.e., they're all risk takers. That was certainly the case with the priests in our study. They are active, enthusiastic, and energetic. They have a willingness to look life straight in the eye. Most know how to accommodate change, but, more than that, many positively thrive on change. "Without change," said Art, a 47-year-old Southern priest, "I think we are dead, basically." Harry, a 44-year-old Southern pastor who has had a number of different ministries in his priesthood, said "I'm tired of packing. I want to settle down for a little bit. But because I'm tired of packing doesn't mean I'm tired of changing."

Priests talk about change and excitement interchangeably. Dick, 62, a Southern pastor who was the oldest priest in the four focus groups, reflects on his life as a "change agent." He said, "I am never satisfied that I have conquered all the hills that God has put in front of me. I am always looking for a new one to climb. And that has been tremendously life-giving throughout my life....I think the bottom line of it all, though, is being the change agent. That to me is what has given me the biggest challenge and made the juices flow. When I look at something, I see it like Robert Kennedy — I look at things and most people say, Why? And I say, Why not, why not? And that just invigorates me to be able to say let's push that horizon a little bit further and look beyond the wall."

The image that Dick used was that of the Israelites taking the risk to leave Egypt. And when change isn't working out so well he said that we have to resist "the temptation to go back to Egypt, or back to where we were."

Another pastor from the South put it this way: "Too many people don't want to enter the process of change because they don't want the pain. To get somewhere, to make some progress you are going to have to die a little bit."

A third pastor from the South talked about the power of perseverance to effect change. "If I really believe in something, I just keep doing it. There is some credibility that is built up in me, if nowhere else, that I am being faithful to what I am trying to live out. I find that effects change."

Peter, 53, another Southern pastor and former director of continuing formation of clergy, sees the status quo as a wake-up call. In 27 years of priesthood "I have enjoyed being on the razor's edge, always pushing it back just a little bit further," he said. "I think that produces life. I think one of the most debilitating things for me would be to sit in a rut and not change."

Peter even finds change life-giving when it brings suffering; he described the lessons he learned from problems with deteriorating vision.

> Over the last two or three years I've had trouble with my eyesight and am very much visually impaired at this point so that I no longer drive at all. Most of what I have to read I have to read by magnifying glass or by enlarged print. What I do takes me twice as long as it used to. And it is forcing on me a dependency upon God and upon other people that is very difficult because I've been a very independent person.
>
> It is not welcome and I would be lying if I sat here and said, 'Yes, it's welcome and I celebrate it, enjoy it.' It's not true. But I do in my saner and more faithful moments recognize the value of that change and recognize that even though I don't know where it's going, it will lead to something that, yes, I can manage and, yes, I can deal with. Perhaps it will even make me a better person than I am because I have lots of things about me that I don't like and that other people don't like either. And, specifically, I think it has brought me closer to some people because they see in the suffering something that they can also recognize in their own suffering.

Joe, 51, a diocesan official from the West, said it's exciting to help people in times of crisis. "I have in my parish a couple of people who are fire fighters and they love it because of the excitement," he said. "When that phone rings and they have to respond, they are pumped up and they love it. I would say in some ways there is an adrenaline rush with us, too, and I think that pumps us up. It's called an addiction. It's an endorphin rush that we are addicted to."

Rick, 43, a Western chancery official, said:

> For me, the greatest satisfaction about being a priest and being in the Church is when we are doing things. When you say, 'This is what Jesus calls us to do, it's what the Gospel is all about,' we are doing it. We are in the forefront. We are on the cutting edge and, you know, we don't have to explain what we are doing because you can just look at it and see what we are doing. That I find life-giving. But if we are always in a reactive mode, that could just wear you down.

Jeff, 41, a chancery official from the East, notes that while he presently lacks the day-to-day parish experience, he also has a feeling of excitement about the Church and his work:

> I think what's been life-giving to me and a blessing, has been to really get a vision of what the Church is called to be and to challenge other people to a deeper sense of that vision....I don't share in parish ministry now. But I do share in the excitement of getting a glimpse of the vision of something exciting that's happening in a parish or in another diocese or another part of our country. To be able to somehow challenge the local diocese, the local parish, the local people to do better — that to me is extremely exciting.

Some priests talked about the difficulty of changing assignments and leaving people. Roy from the South struggles with goodbyes, mourning and grieving, but sees "that death-resurrection thing is part of what it means to be alive and to be human. Change will take place and it's not so frightening." He sees the wisdom in a pastor having a certain tenure in a particular parish: "I like that sense of moving on, picking up the tent, living nomadically, finding the presence somewhere else in new people."

Within the space of a year, Peter's mother and sister died. They had been very close; they would often spend his day off together. "That was a devastating change for me at the time because it meant a whole pattern of life had changed," he said. "But in going back and looking at it, the change in family life opened me up to more people and to other possibilities."

Education is also an important part of change. Peter, who has five college degrees, said, "I've always been curious. I want to know what is on the other side of the fence. I'm not satisfied with what I know. I want to expand. I want to be more. I want to do more. I want to know more. And that has been life-giving." Jim from the Midwest said, "Continuing education is important. I continue to take advantage of all the opportunities I can."

As life becomes increasingly more fast-paced, change becomes a constant. These priests don't just cope with change, they thrive on it. The image that seems to be operative here is the biblical image of "setting out." We don't always know the destination or whether it will work out, but we are a people on the move, on pilgrimage. "Set out! I will be with you!" This is God's exhortation to Abraham and Moses; it is an exhortation that continues to be heeded today.

2. Balance, Perspective, and Time

The priests in this study offer a paradox. They are risk-takers, but they also have an incredible sense of balance. They've developed the ability to see limits and boundaries, to avoid giving too much or simply burning out. They come across as a group with solid mental health skills. They also have the ability to see the big picture, judge the pros and cons of a situation, and then make decisions.

Even as priests describe the way that change gives them life, they also talk about the need for stability. Larry, 44, a Southern pastor said, "I need change, but I need it undergirded with some stability. I could not survive in a chaotic situation. I have to have at least one foot touching the ground. One foot can be pretty high up in the air, but one foot has got to be kind of close to the ground."

Art, who said that priests are dead without change, also said:

> In the process, there are some things that have to remain constant even in the midst of change. I think there is great wisdom in that little prayer that asks God to grant us the serenity to accept what we can't change, courage to change what we can, and the wisdom to know the difference. I find that, as I continue to learn that ever more, it takes away a lot of the frustration from my life. Sometimes there are things that we cannot change and until we come to recognize them, we can wind up being very frustrated.
>
> I always have to start with the premise that I cannot change somebody else. To put it kind of bluntly I suppose some of it would be dealing with our bishop. In some sense, early on, it was

a kind of frustration for me that he wasn't perhaps a little bit different than he is. But I am coming to terms with that.

We have to learn to live with the gap. There is always going to be a difference between who I am and what I'm called to be. There have been priests that I've known who have left, who in many ways have far greater qualities than I have. But when it came down to it, I don't think they were able to live with that gap. I think that in some way that was what led them on the road out. I've read all the books about priesthood, and if you read all of them about what a priest is called to be, it's basically impossible. So you have got to learn to live with the gaps.

The priests' sense of balance often comes from new ways of thinking about life. This story came with a twist worthy of a perverse O'Henry story from Gary, 41, a Midwestern diocesan official. It shows that turning points for priests aren't always dramatic events; most seem more like awakenings, new ways of thinking about life:

An incident comes to my mind from probably ten years ago or more when I was going to a hospital to visit a kid whom I knew fairly well. He was suffering, dying of cancer. I was going to visit about three times a week or more toward the end. And I remember driving back from the hospital after an especially long day at school — I was assistant principal at that time — and watching this kid waste away, spending time with his family and all that sort of thing, I thought, 'Who needs this? This is crazy. Who needs to put up with this kind of crap?'

And so I am driving back and I'm looking in the rear view mirror. I am at a stop light, looking in the rear view mirror and there is this nice, handsome couple behind me. And I thought, 'Look at them. They are so happy. You know, they are really having a great time. They are going home and will have dinner with each other. Probably pick the kids up at day care and have a great evening together and a wonderful life. Just when I was thinking that, in the time it took to wait at a stoplight, all of a sudden the woman reaches over and slugs the guy in the mouth. And I thought, 'Oh, my gosh.' And they got into one brutal fight in their car and I thought maybe it ain't so wonderful. And that was a real good lesson for me. Now I don't want to make too much of that, but it sure had an impact that day and really helped me go into school the next day. Okay, there is a little bit of crap in everybody's life. You learn how to live with it.

One Western priest says, "I go on that old adage that God has given us the gifts and the graces that we have. Our responsibility is just to do the best that we can. And after that it's the Lord's responsibility. So whether it works out or not, at least I try to live with `Well, I did my best.'"

Tim, 42, a high school principal from the West, said he doesn't want to "overreact to people's anger and to people's negativity because lots of that anger and that negativity I have to remember isn't to me. They had it long before I ever got there. I just happened to be the focal point and if I take it personally and overreact to it, all I do is exacerbate the problem and make it worse."

A priest named Andrew takes inspiration from his namesake:

> One of the things that gives me life I would say is recognition of limits. Using my own namesake in the Gospel, Andrew, might be in some sense an explanation. He doesn't turn up too often. But two of the times he turns up, all he does is introduce somebody else. That is it. He didn't take on the responsibility of converting them. He left that to Christ, but he introduced Peter and he introduced the young fellow with the loaves and fishes. And in some sense I think if I recognize this, I am not called to do everything. That in some sense I'm just called to introduce and we leave it up to God and up to the grace of God after that.

Richard, a pastor from the East in his sixties, talks about the need to respect the "vacuum days" in a new job: "When you are in a new assignment, you are the one person there who knows the least about the situation. So you are in a vacuum. And depending on the size of the parish it takes a certain amount of time to come out of the vacuum. You have to stay in the vacuum. You have to keep yourself in the vacuum. If you jump out of the vacuum while you are still in the vacuum, then you are kidding yourself. You are not seeing the situation."

Balance includes knowing how to take care of yourself physically and mentally. Most priests didn't talk a great deal about physical health, but it was clearly a factor. Several talked about regular racquetball sessions or long walks. But only two of 35 priests appeared to be even slightly overweight, a percentage well below the national average for men in this age group. Charlie from the Midwest spoke of the importance of exercise which he realized after having an angina problem: "I think we have to be healthy. I exercise regularly, at least three times a week for an hour at a physical fitness center. If I don't do it, I get tired. I feel it within myself physically. I can't do the same amount of work that I could yesterday."

A sense of humor is a part of balance. It is also part of the virtue of kindness. Theologian Romano Guardini tells us: "One other thing is required by kindness, something of which we rarely speak, a sense of humor. It helps us to endure things more easily. Indeed, we could hardly get along without it. The person who sees man only seriously, only morally or pedagogically, cannot endure him for any great length of time. We must have an eye for the oddity of existence. Everything human has something comic about it. The more pompously a man acts, the greater is the comic element. A sense of humor means that we take man seriously and strive to help him, but suddenly see how odd he is, and laugh, even though it be only inwardly. A friendly laugh at the oddity of all human affairs, that is humor. It helps us to be kind, for after a good laugh it is easier to be serious again."

All four sessions were frequently marked by laughter. Roy, 40, a Southern pastor, said, "One of the things that has brought me life personally and professionally is a sense of humor. I don't know how you survive if you don't have it. I really don't know how you do it. And it's brought joy to me, but it's also been much more than just a survival tactic. It has been a real gift that I've been able to use." Bill, 40, a Western pastor, offers an example of that sense of humor: "I worked five years on a personnel board and saw the things that people put up with in their priests. On the board we would often say, 'The Lord chose twelve dumb fishermen a long time ago and He continues to do that.'"

Stewards of Time

A common problem for priests is the constant demands on their time. Priests love their work, but they also treasure their time off. Neil, 39, a diocesan official from the East, notes that "What has sometimes been a struggle over the years is the expectation: 'But you are a priest and you are supposed to...' At times I have been real honest with people and just said, 'I recognize that but this is what I can do.'"

Don from the Midwest talked about the attraction of being busy:

> I remember in my younger days, people would ask me 'How are you doing?' And I would say 'Man, am I busy.' And underneath that, I think I was saying to myself and hoping others would say to me, 'You are damn important. You are really important because you are so busy.' Later I would ask guys around the country, 'How are you doing?' And they would say 'Man, I am tired. I'm busting my butt.' That is the theme all around the country these days with clergy.
>
> Well, I came back to the parish bound and determined I was going to learn my limits and live within some limits. And I really have worked at writing a job description for myself, trying to choose what I'm going to do and what I'm not going to do. It's going to be damn important for us to choose what to do and what not to do as the job shifts and changes and possibly expands.

Don said he struggles with one-to-one ministry versus leadership or ministry to the system:

> I used to think that one-to-one ministry was most important. There is no question that it is a potential graced moment. But I believe the hay is made in the system of ministry. Building a system where people can connect with each other, where the values are truly held up, and where people have an opportunity to be who they are. I have decided, for example, to never meet with the same person more than once in a counseling situation. I will talk with them one time, then refer them. And that is a hard decision. In some ways I don't want to make that decision, but that is an example of the kinds of limits that I think you have got to make if, in fact, your primary ministry is a system of ministry.

Don said he received a "pearl" from someone concerning this issue of balance and burn out: "If it is God's work, God will give you the energy. If it is your work, you are probably going to get tired."

Jack, a four-time pastor from the Midwest, echoed Don's comments on busyness.

> This last year on retreat I got hold of the fact that there is something addictive about being so much in demand and so busy. When I walk in the office they are coming at me from every direction. Everybody on the staff wants to see me. The phone is ringing. And you don't get done half of what you want to get done. I began to realize the problem is not the job. The problem is your need

to be there. The place runs fine when you are not there. You can take your time for prayer. It was my need to be needed. It was addictive to me. Is this really the need of this ministry or my need to be in the middle of everything? I go off on vacation for two weeks and come back and everything happened that was supposed to happen. All those phone calls were dealt with. So maybe I don't need to be there as often as I think I do.

The need for time off was a recurrent theme. One priest said, "I consider my day off sacred. I count on that day off as part of what revitalizes me and I try to make it as different as I can from the other six days of the week. I sleep late. I don't say my prayers. I just want a day that is a different routine, totally different."

Al, 45, an Eastern pastor, said:

Yesterday was a beautiful day and I had heavy meetings in the morning and I knew I had several appointments in the evening, and a couple of hours free in the afternoon. I thought, 'I'm going to get out of here. I've got two hours, I'm going to go outside and do something just to enjoy myself' even if it, and it was, raking some leaves. School is out now, you know, and I walked over to the school in a tee shirt and dungarees. One of the school kids said, 'Oh, I didn't know you don't have to wear that black shirt all the time?' I did feel good. Later in the afternoon and in the evening I was back to doing what I needed to do and responding to people. It was a good day.

Don from the Midwest put it this way: "I am very glad

to have the opportunity I have to work and I believe in the work I do. But I thrive on getting out of there."

Peter from the South said,

> Time by myself, time to be alone gives me life. Whether it's time alone in prayer, in traveling, in cooking, in the garden, or in the office just closing the doors for a few minutes, I need the opportunity to simply rebuild and renew myself by stepping back from all the contacts I usually have and taking time for myself to look at things or sometimes to do nothing but vegetate really...It's a very active life, but I also need a life where I have time by myself.

John from the West said, "Sometimes I think some of us get so consumed that we think the Church is the world. There are other things besides ministry. We have to get ourselves in perspective. There is more to this than hanging around the rectory doing good."

The first habit in the best-selling book, *The Seven Habits of Highly Effective People*, is "Be Proactive." We are responsible for our own lives; our behavior is a function of our decisions, not our conditions. The priests in this study have this habit; they are intentional about life. They are available but it is an intentional availability. They are good stewards of their time. This is an effective style of ministry, but it also assumes that "I don't always have to be there for Church to happen or for God to effect anything."

3. Authenticity

Over and over again, the priests in our focus groups

talked about the need to be honest with themselves and with others. These priests want to be themselves. They don't want to just "go through the motions." They are willing to look at themselves honestly. They see their strengths but also their weaknesses and challenges as clearly as they see anything else.

As Gene from the Midwest explained it, "Just don't put on any pretense. Don't be somebody other than what you are. Be yourself in liturgy. Come as you are and help other people come as they are. And, in that way we can pray better. It's when we try to be something other than we are that I think God gets cut out sometimes."

Effective priests are honest with themselves, with their superiors, and with those they serve in ministry. Tom from the West illustrates this concern.

> I think what it comes down to and what the people look for is that they don't really care whether Father is gay or straight. I don't think they really do. They care: 'Is Father authentic? Is Father prayerful? Is Father holy? Does Father live his life according to how he tells us to live?' And that doesn't mean now that Father is going to be perfect, you know.
>
> The people from the pews see us better than we see ourselves. What they look to is: Is this person a person of compassion? When he celebrates the Mass, is he just going through the motions? Or is he really praying? Is he praying not just for us, but also for himself? And does he realize that he needs salvation just as much as we do? That is what they are looking for.
>
> People can recognize whether you are au-

thentic. They can recognize that your call and your vocation and your work is true and honest and that you are doing the best you can. People can deal with human weakness, if there is honesty.

For some, authenticity involves staying close to their roots. "Never forget where you come from" is the advice offered by Fred, whose childhood as the son of working-class Irish immigrants makes him feel comfortable with working-class Hispanic immigrants. Two priests from Louisiana identify themselves as "Cajuns" and take pride in their reputation for stubbornness.

Roy from the South talked about the honesty he found in a Twelve-Step recovery program: "It has been so eye-opening to me because when you are with this group of priests who are all swimming in the same illness, you just can't escape the honesty that we call forth in one another. It's a stark honesty, because we know all the games, all the little tricks of the trade. That has been really life-giving for me over the past three years."

Priests find it important to be honest about their jobs and assignments. Some priests welcome the challenge of a new assignment; for example, two priests in different parts of the country talked about how much they had learned after accepting assignments in jail ministry. But another priest recalls as a major turning point the fact that he turned down an invitation to enter the Vatican diplomatic corps: "I said thanks, but no thanks. There was something in me that said I can't do that. I don't want to do that. That is not where my heart is."

Peter from the South recalls learning to be honest after

he was removed from a parish after a clash with his new bishop.

> The administration changed in our diocese and I didn't get along with them and they didn't get along with me. It was a mutual dissatisfaction and disagreement and I was removed from my parish ministry, which I loved dearly, and told that there was no other parish ministry for me. So there was a whole change in my pastoral way of ministering. It changed how I looked at my priesthood. It changed how I looked at Church. It changed how I looked at other priests and has affected my life since that point in terms of who I am and where I am.
>
> Those two, three, or four years were extremely difficult, he said. "But if nothing else, it taught me the value of honesty and truth. For everything else that I can find bad during that period of administration, the one good thing I keep going back to is that it freed me to be able to walk in to the bishop and say, 'This is what I think of what you did'. Prior to that time I would never have been able to do that. And since that time I am a little bit freer in saying 'This is where I am and who I am. I am willing to listen to you. I am willing to change, if that needs to be. But this is the truth of who I am, where I am, and where I am going.'

Bill from the West describes what he learned about honesty in a difficult parish situation.

> I had to send my associate away this past fall

and I asked him to write a letter to the parish saying, 'I'm going through some emotional difficulties.' It turns out that he is dealing with some manic-depression issues. I knew again in today's climate that if we just sent him away, people would say, 'Who did he get involved with sexually and abuse?' Or the rumor right away was he has a drinking problem. But when he wrote and said 'I am here for issues which I haven't quite sorted out. The priesthood wasn't what I expected it to be and I'm dealing with some issues of depression.' Over the course of his three months, 500 letters went to him supporting him, telling him we love him. The welcome when he got back, the joy of seeing him take some steps, and his example have given people the courage to look at their own lives and say, 'I have got some issues of depression in my own life and if he could deal with it, maybe I can, too.' That is life-giving.

Larry from the South said, "In the last five years I have experienced a change in myself from a role to a person which has been so freeing...I can go to my superior now and just tell him what I think. This inner freedom has been very exciting, challenging, frightening, and risky."

"When it comes to ministry, authenticity means being accountable," Jeff from the East said. "For too long priests perceived that ordination meant you were no longer accountable. One of the reasons why we are sitting here around this table is because all of us probably hold ourselves accountable for who we are and what we do. We need to understand that we are accountable for everything that we say and do, just as much as we hold other people accountable for what they say and do. I heard a couple of horror stories.

As a Church we celebrated Easter. And yet, in how many parishes throughout our country and in our own diocese do guys use that as an opportunity, literally, without even thinking, to chastise those who only show up on Easter and Christmas. Holy s—! There's a tremendous opportunity to welcome people. Guys are not held accountable for what they say."

Bob from the Midwest said, "Another thing that is important to me is truth. 'The truth will make you free.' I think for me priesthood is largely a matter of allowing people to speak the truth about themselves and what is in their hearts. There is something very powerful that goes on when people can do that. And it reminds me of my own quest to be truthful with God, with myself, with other people."

Effective priests know who they are and are comfortable with who they are. Honesty with superiors, the people they serve, and themselves is a core element of what makes them effective and free.

4. A Life of Multiple Intimacies

The Catholic priesthood requires celibacy, a life without sex or marriage, and for some priests, this leads to a life of loneliness. But to the priests in this study, celibacy does not preclude warm friendships and intimate relationships. Some of the priests in this study even speak of the freedom that celibacy gives them to have more such relationships than many married people have. In Martin Buber's terminology, they thrive on "I—Thou" relationships which enable them to be more effective, helping, healing, enabling, and loving.

Family

People form their first relationships within their families, and family life is important to priests. There is a tendency to think of families primarily in terms of providing support to young men in their decision to enter the priesthood, and that support is clearly important. But our focus groups also make clear that their families — parents, aunts, uncles, brothers, sisters, nieces, nephews, cousins — are important to priests throughout their priesthood. These priests visit their families, spend holidays with them, and get involved in their lives. One priest has gone on vacation with his mother. Another has grown close to a first cousin and a second cousin who live nearby. One priest says his family keeps him honest: "My brothers and sisters don't take anything from me just because I am a priest. My parents do a little bit. But not my brothers and sisters."

Several priests recalled the family life that had shaped them. Phil, 53, a Midwestern pastor, said, "My Dad always was the quiet one, but he had a very dry sense of humor. My Mom had a laugh that was recognizable in any large room. She was very strict, a tough disciplinarian. But we did things as a family. I have a younger brother who has cerebral palsy. He was born with that and he became the focus of the family because he needed help walking. He wore braces and they said he would never be able to walk or talk. He had a wheelchair at two years old. But through physical therapy and speech therapy he graduated from high school. He drives a car. He has a job today. He's been my inspiration. But, the family commitment to that was a big factor."

Two priests described their strong connections to dead brothers. Jim from the Midwest learned to appreciate the gift of life when his older 16-year-old brother died. Art from the South said: "I have an older brother I never knew. And yet from comments of my parents I learned that even though I never knew him, he knows me. There is a bond or a connection there."

These priests learned commitment from their families. While we asked only about the marital status of our priests' parents, many volunteered the length of time their parents had been married, and there was more than one Golden Anniversary among them. Mike, 42, a high school principal from the West, described learning about commitment from his father.

> I always thought since I was a little kid I would love to grow up and be as wise as my father. He said very little. I come from a large family of ten kids. My Dad struggled to make it and send us through school and his wisdom basically was that his sights were always set beyond. He always saw the horizon and it was always rooted in an incredibly deep faith, no matter what. I guess that inner strength is where I get my basic strength. My Dad relied on the Lord consistently, no matter what. When he got married, my Mom's father said 'You want to marry my daughter? Well, how are you going to do it?' And he said, 'Look, as long as I have these two hands, she will never starve. She will always have a roof—as long as God helps me use these two hands.' I have just admired that kind of incredible strength my whole life and my Dad is still the same today. He, for me, is my most fundamental basic supporter. And it's been an incredible source for me.

Tom, 48, a Midwestern pastor, talked about how, when he was in the second grade, he learned forgiveness from his father. Tom's mother was going out to play bridge; she told the children that they didn't have to take baths that evening. When Tom's father came home, he didn't believe the children and made them take their baths. Tom related:

> Later that night, it must have been about one o'clock in the morning, Dad woke us all up and he got us all in the room and he said, 'I want to apologize to all of you. I made you do something. I didn't believe you.' Well, that was the first experience I ever had of being asked to forgive someone. I guess I had asked somebody to forgive me a lot of times, but no one had ever asked me to forgive them, especially an adult and especially my Dad who couldn't make a mistake and here he was telling us at one o'clock in the morning he made a mistake. And he didn't want to wait until the next morning. He wanted us to know it that night. To be honest, I don't like confession in the Church. But I've got to tell you, my priesthood is wrapped around forgiveness and being forgiven. To me that is what it is about. I am constantly in need of being forgiven and there is an awful lot of opportunities out there for me to forgive and helping to lead people to do that. And it stems from that moment with my Dad.

Priests must respond to challenges within their families. Don, another Midwesterner, found that out when his alcoholic brother required assistance and Don had to help raise his brother's five children. Phil from the Midwest described what happened when he learned that his sister was a lesbian.

My youngest sister, who is sort of the joy of my life, is about 11 years younger than I am. She came out of the closet about two years ago. So my life has gotten very interesting because I often find myself in the Southern city where she lives in a lesbian community where I'm not used to being. But I'm getting better at it each time I go down there. And I found a use for myself there. It has been kind of interesting. It has added a different kind of perspective to my life and to my ministry. My oldest sister who still lives on the East Coast is quite mystified by all this, but I've been able to be a bridge between the two of them, to open them up to continuing a good relationship.

Jim, 47, a pastor and diocesan official from the Midwest, described the family tensions that emerged when his mother objected to the fact that his two sisters both planned to marry divorced men. Jim supported his sisters. "I felt I had to do what I felt was the Christ thing to do at that time," he said. "So at that moment it was a negative. Family was kind of a negative. It was putting tension and pressure on me. All that got straightened out, thank goodness, as years went on. But I felt privileged that I could be part of that healing ."

Other Priests

It's not surprising that the friendship and support of other priests is important to these priests. Many of them make a point of having dinner with priests who are friends. One priest shares a weekend cottage with four other priests. Al, 38, an Eastern pastor makes weekly fishing trips with other priests throughout the spring and summer. "On Thursdays," he said, "we'll get six to ten priests who will meet at a restaurant and then go fishing in the afternoon. I don't think that many priests take days off with other priests consistently. Some of us go out and read and walk the mountains, or sit around and tell jokes or swap stories or homilies. But it seems the first two weeks of the spring you get a lot of complaining. It's like breaking that crust. And from then until the end of October, you seldom hear any complaining or griping. It's just that everybody is glad to be out there."

Jack from the Midwest said, "I have always lived in a rectory with other priests. And I don't look forward to the day when I will live alone in a rectory. The relationships have been varied. Some have been satisfying, some have been not so satisfying. But just to live with another priest and to be able to come back from a meeting or from the hassle of the day and to be able to meet, to talk about that, helps me get rid of it and helps me go on to whatever I've got to do next."

John from the West mentioned three older priests who had an impact on his life early in priesthood: "They would be nurturing me and affirming me in my own way of doing things. And I just felt very fortunate to have good, healthy, effective, excited, older men to be around and be nurtured by."

Eric from the South also talked about the good modeling he has had from older priests: "I just admire the strength of their stance and the courage that they have shown over the years. I've tried to pattern myself after the goodness I see in them. I'd like to have the courage I saw displayed in them, in their willingness to stand firm in their view of

Church and to try to live it out...like dealing with racism or even dealing with the administration of the diocese in terms of fairness and theology. And one priest, in particular, has been a model of suffering. Things have not always gone well with this priest in his life, but what a model of generosity he is!"

But if priests value the friendship of other priests, they also react very negatively to priests they see as angry or apathetic. Al from the East said, "I was in a living situation with a fellow priest who was a gardener. He was the pastor and after gardening he would frequently walk back to his room and sit in his room all day. He might have been reading books or watching television or something. But as far as going to hospitals or shut-ins or grammar school or CCD, that was a nonexistent issue in his priesthood. It makes it difficult for others."

Fred, a Western chancery official, said, "I enjoyed a period where I was involved in continuing education with clergy, being able to go to workshops and being around people who are competent. It rubs off. You look around and say, jeez, I am part of this group? I am a peer to this? These are people I would like to be like and that gives me a sense of competency. I dread sitting around with the losers of the diocese. You wonder what gives them energy — booooooring."

Fred also had a complaint about some priests who leave. "We have missed so much, too," he said, "when our fellow priests have left and have not told us the truth, have not done the real relationship thing of writing us and letting us know why. They don't have to give us all the details. They disappear and it's like they didn't matter then and they don't matter now. And that cheapens our life together."

One priest complained about the difficulty in finding a pastor to replace him as he was being transferred out of an inner-city parish. He told the diocese: "The priest doesn't have to be black, just somebody who is excited about life and has some energy. And they said, "Well, we don't have anybody.""

Support Groups

A number of priests also find support groups life-giving. Some are in Alcoholics Anonymous or related groups, while others are in groups of priests who simply come together for mutual support. Jim from the Midwest began early. "I have been out of the seminary for 22 years," he said. "After ordination, I did not want to become an old fart priest and I didn't want to become an alcoholic. And thank God I didn't. I didn't think I had that problem at the time and I wanted to do everything I could to avoid it, so one of the first things I did was join a priest support group and I've been in a priest support group for 20 years. It has been helpful for me. I have been part of three different groups and probably have been in the present group about ten years. We have dealt with some heavy things in our group. There have been tears. We have lost some guys in the group, but to me that has been a very important part of my priesthood, to keep me honest in my endeavors."

Two Western priests had similar experiences. Tom said, "I've been in a support group for 13 years now and I love the wonderful way in which we are able to listen to each other and help each other get through crises because we've all had them at different times. Fortunately, it hasn't been all at the same time so we can deal with one person and then move on."

Bill said, "I have been a member of a priests' support group for 12 years, to be able to bare my soul with someone else who will understand, and to hear, 'Oh, yeah, I went through that.' Or, 'Why don't you try this?' Or, 'We are going to love you.' To have the intimacy of a group that you can just be yourself with and not be judged, to have the comfort of knowing they accept you and love you as a manifestation and a concrete reminder of the Lord's love. That has been so important. I so often see these lonely guys who get angrier and angrier and turn everyone off and you realize they don't have the support or they have locked out everyone from being intimate with them. And we all suffer because of it."

One priest described his experience coming to terms with being the grandchild of an alcoholic. He used a support group to come to terms with the impact his grandfather's alcoholism had had on his mother and what that, in turn, did to him. Ken, 44, a Southern pastor, passed on a lesson from his support group to help others: "I think what has given me life has been a twelve-step program. I am from a dysfunctional family which I guess is pretty common today. And that awareness of how I was many times playing out things that had happened to me in my childhood is very painful. I use three images that have really helped in my ministry called 'Uncover, Recover, Discover.' I have to uncover my history and then recover it. I have to be able to heal those parts of me, so that I can move forward to discover who I am now. And then once I am in the position to love myself, then I can move on to love my neighbor and love the Lord. But I can't go backwards."

Laymen and Laywomen

These priests value the friendship of laymen and lay-women, who often provide honesty and support in their relationships. Several priests talked about having friends for 20 years or more from when they were growing up. Gary, 41, a Midwestern priest who works in the chancery, described some close friends. "I have a group of friends from where I spent the first part of my priesthood," he said, "and they are the kind of people who will tell me 'Where the hell did you get an idea like that?' Or 'That is the dumbest thing I ever heard.' They can be brutally honest with me and me back at them. And we can have some beautiful arguments and some really wonderful arguments. I appreciate that very much. They help keep me human. They help me to not wear this priesthood as a way to distance myself, but rather to help me to relate to people."

Mike from the Midwest said, "Early in my priesthood I tried a priest support group and it just wasn't for me. I found it too negative. All they did was talk shop and bitch about their pastors, and I don't need this. So I chose not to go back. I find most of my affirmation and support in the priesthood through lay people."

Several priests say it's important to have some friends who are not Catholic. One Western priest said, "Some of my best support comes from non-Catholics because they just treat me as Bill. They have been enriched by my priesthood and they celebrate it. But they also celebrate who I am as a person and they give life to that. And there are many people along the way that do that." Rick, a Western chancery official, echoed that view. He said, "Friends who are not tied in with religion enabled me to get out of the role of being just priest and making sure that my identity is Rick. It's not to dichotomize the priestly role and myself. I think they are all one. But still I can say, yeah, this is Rick and I have a life. These friends and family are the ones who keep my feet on the ground."

Married couples and their families play a key role in the lives of many priests. Tim from the West said,

> I just have a whole slew of couples — husbands and wives and families and kids — that I continually keep in touch with and it's very healthy. They know I am Father, but they also know I am Tim, and it's not just talking about ministry always. It's not always just talking about my problems. It's just sitting down and having a good time, having dinner, talking about politics, talking about a trip or this or that. It's being treated as a real person. People sometimes don't treat us like real people.

Tom, 41, a Western chancery official, says he has gained a great deal by staying close with men he knew in the seminary but who left and later married. "The other support system that is really valuable for me has been of couples," he said. "Many of them were guys who were in the seminary with me and left either before being ordained or left after ordination and are now married. I thought it always curious that I feel closer to their wives than I do to them after all of these years. The wives seem more interested in me as a person than the husbands are. But what has been a real good support for me is just being able to be in their homes and getting to know their children and spending time with them. It's a real quality kind of time that I enjoy, especially the conversations we get into with the wives."

Similarly, Dick, a 61-year-old Eastern pastor said, "There's a guy whom I met in my first assignment and his background was quite similar to mine in a lot of ways, so we really became tight. We knew the type of person we had hoped he would marry. He had a lot of offers but not the right type. So we really prayed for the right one to come along, and she came along. I knew it before him. And they did marry, they have six kids now. It's real neat. It takes me through all the family process."

Women Friends

These priests have men friends and couple friends; they also have very close female friends. One focus group was remarkable for its candid discussion of these relationships. One speaker raised the subject, and the next four talked about their own relationships with women.

The first priest to talk about his relationship with a woman said, "I have a woman who is part of my life and a religious sister. I try to keep that as a celibate and honest thing and it's no small matter. But it is very, very rewarding to me to be able to have somebody I can just be myself with and talk with and all."

These comments came from different priests in the group:

- "I am blessed by the relationships I have with people. I have one friend in particular with whom I am very close. My celibacy means a lot to her. It means a lot to me. And she is married, has a number of children. But it's a life-giving relationship and without it I wouldn't be the priest that I am."

• "From the time I was a seminarian to the present, I've always had a close female friend. It hasn't always been the same friend. Circumstances and things have changed. But I think that relationship is very life-giving to me. The person who is a friend of mine is a sister. She wants to be a sister. I want to be a priest. Neither one of us has any desire to be something other than that. And so you still have to deal with the issue of celibacy and affection and all that, but that relationship is a big part of what is life-giving to me. She brings another dimension to me, the female response to me and to my issues and to my life. I think that is very enriching."

• "I've always had very significant friends. And for myself, too, there usually has been a woman who has been a significant person. And that has been a struggle, but I find that it's real important for me to touch in upon the feeling level of myself and, by and large, women help me do that so much better than men do. I am in a priest support group and we don't cry much. We talk about stuff and we are fairly honest with each other. But do we touch on the feeling level? Not much. But if I am talking with a good friend who is a woman, there is a much better chance that she is going to help pull that stuff out and maybe vice-versa. And I need that or else I start drying up. I need to feel it, pain or joy. I need to feel it. And that helps a lot."

• "I, too, have had two personal relationships with women. The first one came early in priesthood.

You are locked up in this seminary for 11 years. You get out and, wow, you know, that was an experience. But thankfully she was happily married and I was just still new enough in priesthood not to do anything stupid. But it was my first time that I experienced being involved. During the seminary we weren't allowed to date, of course. I went into seminary my sophomore year of high school so there was no prom for me. There was no dating. We couldn't be lifeguards. There was a whole big set of rules that we weren't allowed to do. And then all of a sudden, bang, you are out there. But I appreciated the experience. I am still very close to that family. And I thank God that I didn't do anything stupid.

The second relationship has been with a religious sister. I have been a lot better in that one because, again, there is a common commitment or understanding of what this celibacy thing is all about. Even though it's difficult, there is an understanding. You try to talk to a lay person about what celibacy is all about, especially a woman that you are kind of fond of, it's very difficult to get that across. So I have learned more from a love relationship with a religious sister than I did from my first experience.

The priests in this study don't let a life of celibacy turn into a life of loneliness. They live lives of multiple intimacies through close relationships with family, other priests, religious sisters, laymen, laywomen, and married couples. Those relationships give them life.

The impact of intimate relationships came across in the focus group in the South, which reflected Louisiana's fascination with tombstones as an art form. Dick, 62, talked about the epitaph he would like on his tombstone, and it is one that many priests could accept. "I think I saw this in one of Van Zeller's books in the monastery, but it has become my personal motto," he said. "A lot of people are responsible for making sure this is on my tombstone. And if it's not, there will be a lot of people I am going to haunt. But to me it sort of summarizes everything. It summarizes all the things we talked about today. It has a way of being pertinent to everything — marriage, celibacy, priesthood, life, and it is French. Freely translated, it says, 'You really haven't loved if it hasn't brought some suffering. And you are stupid to suffer unless it is because you love. But if you suffered and loved rightly, you are going to be able to die singing.'"

5. Significance of Priesthood and the Mystery of the Call

Another pattern that became apparent in these priests' lives was their conviction that being a priest was a significant way to spend their lives, and that the call to that way of life was a mystery and a gift.

Gary, a Midwestern chancery official, said, "I remember being asked one time why I was in the seminary. And without thinking about it I said, 'Because I believe in the power of the Gospel to change people's lives for the better.' And I really hadn't given much thought about it until that question. But that sentiment has been consistent throughout that seminary time and throughout my priestly ministry. A college kid one time on a retreat was giving a talk and said that there is nobody who is more powerful than a priest, and

I thought, 'What in the world does he mean by that?' And he went on to explain the opportunity to address and influence hundreds and maybe thousands of people every weekend and to say something significant in their lives."

Another Midwestern priest said, "My dad was a salesman and he sold cookies. It seems to me that in some sense we've got the best thing to sell in the world. We have life and love and the Gospel and our big job is to believe in that and get out of the way. And raise that up."

Dick, a current pastor in the South and a former chancery official, related that his father thought he was blaspheming to think a Cajun could be called by God. Today, Dick says, "It gave me life to be able to say to God, 'I think You are calling me,' when my pastor didn't think so, when my father didn't think so."

Jack from the Midwest recalls a return visit to his high school. He was looking at the pictures of the classes who had graduated from his high school and thinking that not one boy in that school wanted to be a priest. "And I did," he said. "And I couldn't understand why. I can't tell you why I felt the way I did. My parents tell me that I said I was going to be a priest at 5. Well, I said it then. I said it 20 years later. I'm saying it 25 years after having been ordained. I want to be a priest."

One priest recalled coming to the United States with the boat people from Vietnam in 1975. He told the story of being in a refugee camp in Pennsylvania when a priest asked if there was anyone in the camp who was a seminarian and who wanted to continue to become a priest. He described his response as instinctual and certainly out of character. "I don't know, I just raised my hand. I was the first one to raise my hand."

Gene from the Midwest said, "I can't imagine a life in which my gifts could be used more. When I look at the gifts that God has given me and then I look at the life of the priest, it just fits."

One priest describes his sense of call this way: "I think what has kept my juices going all these years is that towards the end of high school, I felt a call and I continue to feel that, a sense of mission and wanting to live my life in such a way that is of service, of trying to make a difference."

Don, 48, a pastor from the Midwest, describes priests as "walking symbols." He said, "What goes on with us is way beyond our personalities and our talents. We are walking symbols in some ways. And it's a lot bigger than me and what I've learned in my education. I don't know how to balance it. I spent a lot of the early years in my priesthood trying to be one of the people — 'I am a plain old person like all the rest of you. I struggle like all the rest of you.' And there was something holy, I think, in that. But there is another side of that truth and there is almost a shaman kind of a dimension to what we do. We are walking symbols."

Jack, 54, a pastor from the Midwest recalls feeling a sense of mission while overhearing a group of Kentucky Fried Chicken executives talking on an airplane.

> There was this unbelievably animated conversation. The whole conversation had to do with chicken. And these people, their whole life was into this and they were excited about it and I'm sure KFC loved having them on the staff. And at some point it just came to me and I said, 'Oh, I'm so glad I have something more significant than chicken to offer.' I think the Gospel is life and

death. It brings a level of meaning to the world of chicken and whatever. And if that meaning isn't brought to that world for other people, myself, whomever, then I think it is kind of shallow. And to be able to provide a foundation, a depth for people, that to me is very exciting.

Dick from the South said, "I deeply feel that a tremendous amount of what Jesus preaches is what the world needs. And it certainly is life-giving to me to know that I can help people be aware of that truth. And so I feel very blessed and very privileged to know that somehow I help keep those Gospel values alive."

Bob, 39, a Midwestern educator, related a vivid awakening he had had into the significance of his priesthood:

I was having doubts for a while about whether I wanted to continue in the priesthood. "I have two brothers and six sisters, all of whom are married, and I was sitting there one night and was kind of daydreaming, contemplating. And I remember thinking, what is it that my brothers are doing as married men that I am not doing. And all of a sudden I thought — one never knows where these thoughts come from — when they make love to their wives they give them a gift, and we call it semen, the Latin word for seed. And that seed that they give, that they plant can mingle with the gifts that their wives bring to that act and new life can come about. And I kind of jumped up in the chair and said, holy s—! What am I supposed to be doing? That's it. That is what I am supposed to be doing, planting seeds in other people's lives that mingle with the gifts that they bring to the relationship so new life can come about.

I got so excited. I went out and ran a couple of miles. I don't know where it came from, but it's a very powerful image in my life now. I want to be a priest. I love my priesthood, but when people ask me why I am a priest, I am sometimes tempted to say, it's like somebody asked Louis Armstrong, 'Tell me about jazz. What is jazz?' And he said, 'If you have to ask the question, you ain't ever going to understand the answer.' I remember an article in Time magazine a few years ago about a French acrobat who gets arrested every time he goes to New York because he throws a wire across the World Trade Center towers and walks. And somebody asked him, 'Why do you keep doing this? You get arrested. You are paying all these fines.' And he said, 'You know, if I see three oranges on the table, I have got to pick them up and juggle. And if I see two tall buildings, I have got to walk between them.' And that made as much sense to me as any explanation of why I am a priest. That is who I am. And I don't know what else to say. I get speechless about it when I look at everything. All I can say is I love it. I love it all, the crazy s—, the goofiness, the shadow side of the human heart, but also all the tremendous good that is there and the Spirit that somehow keeps it all together.

6. God's Love

Attached to the sense of the mystery of God's call is a

sense of closeness to God, of being loved by God. One priest cited the image of God as the "Fiddler on the Roof" who is always there. Roy, 40, a Southern pastor, says "God never sees us or sees me as anything less than wonderful". He said his motto through the years has been, "Just 'Emmanuel'— God is with us!" An Eastern priest talked about his spirituality as a "real energizing relationship with the Lord."

Gary from the Midwest described feeling "graced." He said, "I think that there is a spirit of gratitude among many of us, a sense of having been blessed and graced and, therefore, wanting to share that with other people. People who feel cheated in life aren't usually prone to be generous with their lives. I think there is a sense among us of recognizing how God has moved in our lives maybe in ways that don't make sense to us, and in ways that we wouldn't have planned. Yet we have a real spirit of gratitude of having been blessed, and then want to share that with other people."

Gene, 42, a Midwestern chancery official, describes a "cat-and-mouse" relationship with God. "I think sometimes my relationship with the Lord over the years has been a cat-and-mouse game and I play hide-and-seek sometimes," he said. "There is a different spirit about my ministry when it flows out of a true belief that God loves me. There is less of a frantic sense. There is more of a sense that at the bottom God and I are okay and that we are together.

Tim from the West talked about the busyness of priesthood and getting involved in people's lives and what "grounds" him is "a deep, abiding constancy." He said,

> I've come to a real sense of peace and a deep sense of prayer and a real deep relationship with the Lord that I can depend on. This deep rela-

tionship with the Lord gives me life. I know that no matter what happens and no matter how bad things are going with the Church or in the newspapers or the disgruntlement of certain people, or priests leaving, it doesn't affect me at the core of who I am. And that keeps me going. It gives me the ability to continue to be hope-filled and to spread that.

Peter, a Southern pastor whose failing eyesight is causing changes in his life, talked about God. "Each day I discover more and more and it's becoming boring in my preaching because it gets repeated as I preach it to myself ... and that is the realization that God has loved me first and what I am doing all through my life is responding to that love. No matter what happens, God is going to take care of me. God will provide. God will operate. As I lose my independence and become more dependent, God is going to take care of me. I may not like the way He takes care of me, but He is going to do it.

"What roots me is that I am a sinner and I know I am a sinner and each year I recognize how much of a sinner I really am and God has forgiven me. And if He can forgive me, then He can forgive anybody else no matter how bad I judge them to be."

A Vietnamese priest says that his getting through the seminary in four years was God's work. "I didn't know a word of English," he said. "Every night I had to stay up until one or two in the morning because I had to look up in the dictionary in order to understand all the words...God helped me because I trusted Him and I told Him every day, 'I do my best and You are going to take care of the rest!'"

7. Relationship with Jesus and the Paschal Mystery

While these priests see God as a source of love, they see Jesus as a model. For these priests, Jesus didn't come to lay a guilt trip on people. His proclamation of the Kingdom and his parables offered the people a different way of looking at things, a different world view. Rick, a Western priest, said, "When I was at this one parish, the question was, 'Well, how do I carry out the ministry here?' Even though I was in residence, I was in the tribunal at that time as well. And the question would be, 'What would Jesus do?' It seems simplistic, but I think it's a very appropriate question for a priest to ask. And where do I find that? I look in the Gospel and I find that Jesus ate and drank with those who the public considered to be sinners. And there seemed to be an analogy there. Did Jesus say 'This is the story, this is what I come to teach and you are all wrong and there is no more discussion,' or something like that? That is not what He did. He sat down and talked about their lives. And that is what I found liberating in the Gospels."

Tim from the West said that all of his mentors came up short. He said it wasn't surprising since he himself often came up short. He said that that forced him to realize "there is really for me only one mentor and that is the Lord....there is a consistency of compassion, a consistency of love, a consistency of wisdom."

Dick from the South described undergoing a dramatic change at a workshop on Vatican II at Notre Dame University in 1976. It had to do with his understanding of Jesus Christ. "I had been fighting Vatican II. The highlight of the whole workshop was a course on Christology. I was the only

Southerner at the workshop. Here I am a white Southern boy and in walked Father Ed Braxton, a black priest fresh off the campus of Harvard. He said, "I've come here to challenge your operative Christology" and he did. He put me in touch with the humanity of Jesus that I had denied. And that put me in touch with my own humanity. I was trying to imitate the divine Jesus and denying the human in me because that was not Jesus. That insight gave me life because it made me aware that I had subjugated my humanity, my personality. The training we had had tried to make us all alike and hide our identities behind everybody wearing the same clothes. It was tremendously freeing for me to realize that I could be different and still be good. This helped me an awful lot in my acceptance of black people, of women, of ethnic differences, and of ecumenism. That was very, very freeing. It still is."

Paschal Mystery

The priests in this study also talked about their relationship with Jesus Christ in terms of the Paschal Mystery, i.e., His dying and rising. Just as our salvation was accomplished through Jesus Christ dying and rising, these priests often experience themselves and others moving through death to new life. This might also explain why they find change so exciting. Involvement in the mystery of new life that comes out of death animates these priests.

John from the West talks about going to pieces when he was twelve years old over the death of a grand aunt with whom he had been very close. "I just learned that you are going to survive," he said. Now as pastor, he has had to fire two principals, had people embezzling from the parish, pickets out in front of church. "I just get back to believing in the resurrection of Jesus Christ. I shall rise again. We will make it through."

Frank, 52, a Southern pastor, said,

> For me the most life-giving reality is the Paschal Mystery. The community I belong to stresses very strongly the Paschal Mystery and the reality of passing over, that we pass over from who we are and what we are and empty out into other people's lives and other people's cultures. And so six weeks after ordination I did just that. I ministered for 25 years in the African-American Catholic Church here in the country and the experience of the faith life of the people is a mystery of faith. Why they remain and still do so within the American Catholic Church is strictly a mystery of faith. It's as mysterious as the Paschal Mystery to me. And that has fed me and constantly gives life to me.

Larry, 44, a Southern pastor, said, "The Paschal Mystery is continual. There are new aspects of me that I become aware of. I know that I have to die to certain parts of myself. I have to go into that tomb. But now that I've gone through it enough, I know that there is resurrection at the end. It's not just the resurrection. It's the Paschal Mystery."

Gene from the Midwest said death and resurrection give life. "The closer I see it in people's lives and my own life, it just takes on more and more meaning," he said. He talked about the past three months being very hard for personal and work-related reasons. "And I guess I am slowly learning that it's in dealing with some of that stuff, that life starts springing out, and God is very much present."

8. Spiritual Life

The priests in our focus groups have strong spiritual lives. Prayer, scripture, and liturgy nourish and support these priests.

Prayer

"For me the thing that definitely gives life in my priesthood is daily prayer," said a Vietnamese priest. "Because I remember someone said, that when I stop my life of prayer, I begin to give up my life of priesthood. And I constantly everyday have to remind myself about it. Not only remind myself, but I keep that kind of intimate relationship with Jesus in my daily prayer. I have been ordained a priest for 10 years and I've been happy."

Carl, an Eastern priest, said, "Spirituality for me is the real energizing relationship with the Lord through my 30 years as priest." He said his prayer is, "Father, lead me to a deeper, closer relationship with the Lord Jesus, personally and in the community."

Al from the East talked about a "structured spirituality" as a source of energy in his life. He said, "Praying the Office is really important to me."

Don from the Midwest said, "I thrive on having time in the morning. I can sit down in church and say 'What the hell is on my mind? What are my questions? What is going on? What am I mad about? What am I hopeful about?' To be able to be grounded in who I am and who God is for me is a helpful way to start the day ."

Similarly, Jack from the Midwest talked about personal prayer and the kinds of questions he brings to his dialogue with God: "What the hell did I do today and why did I do it? What am I anxious about for tomorrow? Is it a meeting? Is it a confrontation? Is it a presentation I have to do? And then I take that anxiety to prayer. I find that that kind of prayer helps me both integrate what happened and, hopefully, to be peaceful about what's going to happen or what might happen. I usually do my praying late at night. Jesus said, 'Ask and you shall receive.' And, by now, after 27 years I have this whole litany of gifts that from time to time I ask for in prayer. One of the things I had asked for is the gift of prayer. I am always amazed when I find myself being called to prayer after a long day, when I really wouldn't think that I would want to pray. I believe it is that gift of prayer that is calling me to prayer."

These men find life in their relationship with God. They are aware of God's love for them; that seems to be the starting point. Prayer and ministry seem to be a response to God rather than a means to get God to respond to them. It is interesting that their prayer is very much connected with their ministry; their dialogue with God is about their ministry. It is not as though they have the ministry and their spiritual lives separated and compartmentalized. There's a certain synergy: they relate to God out of their ministry and their relating to God seems to energize them for the ministry.

Scripture and Liturgy

"I just can't imagine the past 30 years of my life without the nourishment of Scripture," said George from the East. "I just couldn't imagine what it would be like because it's been just so constantly enriching. You never go back to Scripture that you don't find something and learn something if you keep working at it. Talk about something that's been sustaining, and that really supports you and makes you stay alive! To have to deal with the Word of God every day and for a large community on Sunday draws so much out of you!"

But George also draws on other sources for spiritual nourishment. "I've rediscovered some of the traditional spiritual classics. I had neglected those for a long time, but there's some wonderful stuff in those things. We had a really interesting session a couple of weeks ago with women on Julianna of Norwich, who is a very interesting woman. We have an incredible and rich tradition of spirituality and of great books. You don't even begin to tap into it. It takes a little bit of work to get at it, but I found a lot of riches there."

Jack, 54, a Midwestern pastor, talked about asking God for the gift of preaching the Word effectively when he was made a pastor. "I just love to preach now. I didn't always. But it seems like it's really not a chore anymore. It's a joy and even when I seem to be coming up dry for five days of the week, on Saturday something seems to come together, maybe that didn't even pertain to what I was reading or looking at. There is a message there that seems to be the right message, if I can just package it right. I have a real sense of that gift being given over and over again."

Some priests stressed the importance of the liturgy in their lives. Peter, 53, a Southern priest said, "I think the first thing that gives me life is involvement in liturgy, beginning with the high point of Easter vigil. It's something that I build up to and something that I draw a lot of experience, a lot of happiness, a lot of celebration out of. But I think it extends to the rest of the year."

Gene from the Midwest said, "Liturgy is becoming more and more important to me. I think in my early years in priesthood I would preside and do things and it was okay.

But as time has gone on, that whole sense of life and sacrament gets closer and closer. Ministry and sacrament need to go together for me. There are times when I am presiding in my parish — I have been there almost nine years, it's a weekend responsibility — that I just start to well up. Part of it is the fact that I look out there and I know almost all of them. Somehow I am there presiding in prayer with them. When I look out during the responsorial psalm and I see parishioners with their eyes closed singing the verse, that just touches me because they are praying, and somehow I am a part of that. I am helping make that happen and praying with them."

Phil, 53, a Midwestern pastor, made a similar comment. "The Eucharist has given my life a certain focus and definition and summation that I need," he said. "When I am sitting up there looking out, I am able to see all the marriages and all the baptisms and all the broken promises and all the divorces and all the single parents and all those that have lost jobs and all those that have found jobs and, somehow either directly or indirectly, I have been there with them. I count how many of them I know. I sit there during Mass and that is quite a challenge because there are sometimes 800 or 900 people there. How many do I know and what do I know them for? I know a lot. And I am grateful for that. That means a lot to me. Sometimes, when I am in between Eucharists, I get weepy and I can't wait to get to my next one."

As the discussion in the Eastern group on what gives life was winding down, Al, a pastor, added, "I'd say one aspect we didn't really cover was the sacramental life of the priest, like confession. I think that is a need. It reminds me of the old story of Damien, the leper. Damien had to stand in the little boat next to the great ship and confess his sins up to the priest on the ship out loud in front of the other sailors because he couldn't come on board. If a priest loses a sense of the need for confession or penance, it's hard to come up with humility, it's hard to come up with generosity."

9. Mystery of God's Activity in Life and Ministry

Early in his priesthood, Rick, now a chancery official in the West, was called to a private home to anoint a terminally ill man.

> I have this problem with allergies and whatever it was in that house — the guy is there dying and he has all sorts of stuff hooked up to him and all — I was sneezing away. All I wanted to do was get out of there. This is a crazy thing. I said, 'Oh, God, I just want to get out of here because I am going to be red and everything else,' and I was already sniffling, not only dripping, but my eyes were watering and all that.
>
> I never met this man before and I got called a few days later that he had died and the family wanted me to do the funeral because that moment was so important to him because he found peace and somehow I brought peace. Well, I wasn't at peace at all. This is my first year after ordination and I thought, well, there is something else going on here besides me.

The sense that "there is something else going on here besides me" is central to what gives life to priests. Many of the priests in our study talked about a sense of mystery of faith and about the power of the Gospel and the power of the priesthood. The theologian, Karl Rahner, said that the greatest pastoral problem in the Church is the "eclipse of mystery." We seem to be out of touch with the mystery of God's activity in our lives. It was obvious that one of the common life-giving factors in the lives of these priests was their awareness that they were part of something bigger than themselves — call it the movement of God, the power of God, or the reign of God. It was clear that for these men there was more to their ministry than meets the eye. Not only was the mystery not eclipsed in these men's lives and ministry, it seemed to give them life.

Their connection to the mystery gave them faith in God's will for them. One priest said, "God works in the unplanned events of the day. That's the Spirit leading us!"

Rick from the West said, "I rely a lot on the Spirit. I find that I really need the Spirit to guide me. The thing about the Spirit is that it's all about fire and courage and letting loose and enthusiasm. I feel myself part of a larger picture, grace, the Spirit's action, or whatever."

Many talked about assignment changes as God's way of challenging them and emptying them. Tim from the West said that because you are competent, you are given more complicated, difficult, and challenging positions. "I find myself, more so now than ever before, having to bring things to prayer because I don't have the answers," he said. "I can't handle this. It is much bigger than me. I have to rely on the presence of the Spirit. Do the best I can. After that, it's the Lord's responsibility."

These priests also have a sense of God's love at work in their ministry. Don from the Midwest put it this way:

"Something is present beyond me. When I'm loving somebody, it's not just me. It's a bigger Somebody."

After a Vietnamese priest's first Mass at his new parish a woman came up to him and said "I am so sorry for you. The people here do not like Vietnamese people." The priest prayed to God, "Okay, you are the one who called me. So I do my best again and you are going to take care of that. I was able to stay there four years. And when I left another lady told me: 'Father, you know you are the priest of the people here. Parishioners have started to like the Vietnamese people here now.'" With God's help this priest became the instrument of reconciliation and inclusion of the Vietnamese people in that parish.

The mystery of God's activity and movement in their ministry is very real for these respected priests. Much like the sneezing young Rick, they feel in touch with something more powerful than they are. They find that power and mystery exciting, and it energizes their priesthood.

These men are also in touch with the mystery of God's movement in their personal lives. While others might see on the surface a tragedy or an inconvenience or an intrusion, these men recognize God's activity. Someone has said that perhaps the most significant function of the priest today is that of "mystagogue," i.e., one who "leads others into the mystery." These priests are able to be mystagogues for the people of God because they are in touch with the mystery of God's activity in their own lives.

10. Drawing Life from the People

Jack, 54, a Midwestern pastor, recalls an incident that

occurred when he was a chaplain at a hospital for the severely handicapped and retarded. "One day I was in the chapel and this little boy walked in, just as happy as he could be. Most people would see him as insignificant. He couldn't speak, he could hardly walk. He had a big smile on his face, and he started to walk by me. And then he stopped and turned around. He came back to me and reached into his pocket and pulled out a gum wrapper, tore it in half, and handed me half and just walked on. And I'm telling you, I never forgot it to this day. The least amount that we give, the more effective it is.

"Two Scripture passages will always be very important to me in my life. The first is about the little boy who gave the fish sandwich to the Lord, and the Apostles said, 'Wasn't that cute?' and patted him on the head and told him to sit down. Now what is the Lord going to do? The Lord said, 'Now, fellows, you sit down. I'll show you what I can do with that.' And the second Scripture passage is about the little old lady walking into the temple with two pennies. Well, all the insignificant gifts are more important because those are the ones that touch."

That anecdote about the little boy and the gum wrapper is just one example of the way in which these priests draw life from the people they serve. They describe a relationship that is synergistic. They draw life from the act of ministry, their ministry enriches people's lives, and the people in turn inspire and breathe life into the priests.

"I think priesthood gives me the chance to be with wonderful people a lot," says Gene, a Midwestern priest. "Last night I had a parish council meeting and there were eleven or twelve of us sitting around the table. We were dealing with all sorts of hum-drum things in a way. But, gosh, the quality of people sitting around that table — people of personal goodness, great people to talk with, deep faith. Time after time, I find that I am privileged to be with people like that."

Bill, 40, a Western pastor, recalls the inspiration he drew from a farewell party as he left a parish: "One of the most life-giving moments was when I left my first parish. I received lots of accolades and a farewell party, and you know they never say bad things, especially when your bag is packed. But someone said, 'Thank you for being our leader, but thank you for not being a leader who was always ahead of us, but for being a leader who walked with us.' And I can only do that because of the life, the care, the trust."

Tim from the South also talked about a farewell party after eleven years of ministry. "I remember going in that room with all these people that I loved so deeply, knowing a lot of their stories, and they knowing me. I wanted to just kind of capture that moment and hold it forever."

Eric, 43, a Southern priest, described being moved by the faith of a new mother with breast cancer:

> Two years ago a woman in the parish had just had a baby, and she was still in the hospital, and was diagnosed with breast cancer. I went to see her that morning and I walked into the room and she was holding this newborn. She looked me in the eye and she said, 'God will be faithful to me.' And what she really meant by that, be- cause she talked about it, was that no matter what is going to happen now, to me or to this child, that God is going to be faithful to me. God is going to take care of this whole thing. She didn't say it in any kind of way as a threat or out of great

theological wisdom, except the wisdom of her experience that God was going to be faithful to her. He would keep his promises to her.

Jeff, an Eastern pastor, said, "It's fascinating just to see so many people who really are believers, who really are active. That, to me, is life-giving. Even though I've been doing it for so many years, I'm not bored, I'm not tired or fatigued, and I thoroughly enjoy parish ministry."

A Western priest talked about his parish which had many gay men and lesbians. A number of his parishioners were dying of AIDS. Ministry to them effected in him a new way of seeing. "An important thing that always gives me life is being a parish priest, because of the life I find from the people, the day-to-day working, the day-to-day lived-out faith in spite of incredible crises at times. They keep the faith. I often say I think I would have run away or cursed God and died or whatever, if I had to face the health crisis. We have buried 26 people that I know of from my parish just from AIDS. The people's lives opened up the Gospels for me. I had to look at them in a different way without all those preconceived ideas and notions."

Art, 47, a Southern priest said, "There was an old lady who lived beside the church where I grew up. Every day of her life she prayed for the priests from the parish. Every day she thought about me when I came to Mississippi. Having someone praying for me everyday is supportive."

Bob from the Midwest said, "I am constantly amazed and surprised by the goodness and dedication of the people with whom I work."

Ken from the South said,

> What I find gives me life most is the rela-
> tionships I have with people in the parish. I really
> love parish ministry, and I think I love it so much
> because of the great privilege I find in the fact that
> people let me into their lives. I am allowed into
> people's sorrows and joys and I feel very inspired
> by their trust. I find the opportunity to get to
> know these people and to love them and to be
> loved back a great treasure.

Bill, a Western pastor, said "In my own life there are
failings and weaknesses. The people know that and yet they
still believe in me, still love me, still say, 'You are the wounded
healer and we are going to give you life because you so enrich
our lives.'" Bob also gets inspiration from the forty or so
people being baptized through the RCIA program in his
parish. "I learn a lot from the neophytes...just to hear what
they believe and what they find so exciting."

George from the East said, "I find a tremendous hunger
among the people for real spiritual nourishment. That's one
of the real challenges for me because they won't let you get
away with not being spiritual. If you are not, they'll just let
you alone. They are looking for meaning and the presence
of God."

Peter, a Midwestern pastor and former chancery official,
recalled a significant moment on a Cursillo retreat weekend
that moved him to tears.

> I remember very clearly one lady coming
> and talking, and at one point in the conversation,
> having a beautiful moment of insight into her life.

> It was like this window just opened up. And I remember I was moved to tears. Whenever I have been able to be part of that journey with someone and you see right before your eyes, maybe it's healing, maybe it's awareness, maybe it's just the sense that they are okay, that somebody cares, maybe the sense that God is really here...if you took away those moments, it would seem empty, I think.

These respected priests also draw life from the great diversity within the American Catholic Church — diversity of race, gender, and even sexual preference. Bill from the West was moved by the diversity in his old parish: "We have a Filipino community. We have a Spanish-speaking community. We are a Heinz 57 variety parish. We have some old Portuguese who aren't delighted that all these people are moving in, and yet through all their pain they keep the faith. Through all their pain you are instantly a member of their family—no matter what your background or your faults or foibles. When they need you, they can share the deepest secrets of their hearts with you and I'm awed by that. That is not just trust in me, Bill, the priest; that is a real trust in the presence of the Lord through me. And that gives me so much life. The gay community, you know, the Church tells them you are rejected, you are ontologically evil, and yet they keep coming back."

A Western priest talked about getting life and energy working cross-culturally in an African-American community. He wondered where he would be spiritually without those Sunday liturgies: "We have a hell of a lot of power and energy and varieties of experiences of God and liberating things that are happening because of the multi-cultural thing here in California. The strength and the vitality that that culture has brought to the experience of Church is a real exciting thing."

Pat, a Southern pastor, adds praise for the example of women religious to his praise of the example of lay people:

> I get a lot of life from the example of religious women. I feel that religious women have given a great deal to the Church, lots of times taking jobs that nobody else wants, at pay and benefits that nobody would work for. They have done an outstanding job, continue to do an outstanding job, that they often will do until the day they die. They are very happy to do it and very effective at it. They have also been a group of people who have consistently tried to increase and further their education and formation and are willing to explore and try a new ideal.

Much of the strength that these priests draw from the laity comes during what they repeatedly refer to as the "key moments," the sacramental moments of birth, marriage, sickness, death, and struggle. Don, 48, a Midwestern pastor and former diocesan official, is experiencing life as a pastor.

> To live in regular dialogue with life and death is a glorious thing to me. Last week I got a call. An old lady died in her chair. Her husband was on the verge of senility, and he just got this dry cry, and to be able to witness the mystery of all that. To just be present for that, and to be there as that is happening, that is awesome to me.
>
> I like to do weddings. There are all kinds of theories among us about weddings and whether

you like to do them or not. But to me it's awesome. People putting their lives on the line. There
is a lot of monkey-business, and it can be a real
pain in the ass, but when you see two people
looking at each other and they are saying 'I am
going to do this forever, I am going to do my
damnedest,' that is awesome to me.

Jack from the Midwest said, "I didn't do a lot of wed-
dings and funerals prior to becoming a pastor five years ago.
But I think it is part of that larger piece that priests have of
being involved in the intimate moments of people's lives. To
be present to people whether it is a wedding or a funeral,
or whether it's a counseling session where people are sharing
their hearts and telling us what their greatest pains and
greatest joys are, there is that element of intimacy that is
very, very satisfying."

John, 48, a Western pastor, said, "I really consider it a
privilege that people allow you into the sacred moments of
their lives. It is such an honor to be welcomed and invited
to be a part of people's lives."

Mark, 43, an Eastern pastor, said, "Recently, I buried
a Sudden Infant Death Syndrome baby. It was the couple's
first child. Everything was going relatively well at the grave
site, everyone was in tears. I was trying to stick to the rite.
That's when ritual is very, very wonderful and very liberating
because it gives you the rhythm to get through this. But the
husband and wife were just hanging onto each other at the
grave site. Then, a week later I got a phone call, and the
father said, 'Father, if you weren't there, we don't know what
we would have done.' So, it's both a sad and a joyful experience."

11. Listening

The experience of being with people at the key moments in their lives has taught these priests the importance of listening. One even has a sign that says "Listen First" on his desk facing him. Other priests make the same point. Jeff, 41, an Eastern chancery official, learned to listen from his sister: "My sister has been a blessing to me. I was a freshman in college when my youngest sister was born. She has what is known as Neunan's Syndrome. She's got motor problems. Now, she's very sociable and can do everything. She calls me every day. But any time that you speak with her you have to listen. You have to just put everything else out of your mind for a minute, and sometimes that's hard. But you've got to listen, and you really have to listen because what she has to say is just as important as any of my other brothers and sisters. And coming from a real Irish background, very extroverted and everything, if there was one skill I probably didn't have growing up, it was the ability to listen."

Don from the Midwest talked about what he did as the new pastor of a parish. "The first two months that I was in this parish, I visited 18 homes where I asked people to bring neighbors together. They got 20 people in a home and I would just keep saying to them, 'Who are you? What is your name? What do you do with your time? What do you like about this parish?' Listen, listen, listen."

Bob, a Midwestern college president, said that listening gives life to his priesthood: "To listen to what is going on in the hearts of other people — I have a sense that I have learned much more from the students I have taught than I have taught to them, and I am supposed to be a good teacher. But there is something that happens when people get together and begin to share the stories that they have, the experiences that they have."

Gene from the Midwest said, "Priesthood for me has always come down to a very concrete life. It comes down to who I am with people, how I pray with people, how I listen to people. How I choose to put as much of myself aside so that I can just be there with them. And in those situations priesthood can be very much alive and powerful."

Jack from the Midwest said, "I think in preaching it is because I listen that I have something to say back to people. Because if I am not listening to what they're saying and experiencing, then I'm not presenting the Word to them in the context of their lives."

12. Service, Compassion, Empowerment

As these effective priests draw strength from being with and listening to people at the key moments of their lives, they feel a duty in turn to be kind and compassionate to the people they serve. Priesthood is not something for the priest; priesthood is for the Church — the People of God. These priests seem to share an underlying assumption that all Christians are called to ministry by baptism and that the priests' real service to a congregation is to help the people realize that. To that end the priest is really serving the movement of the Spirit in the Church. Being in on this movement gives these men life. Leadership for these men involves listening, animating, bringing to life the gifts of the baptized, and helping people realize their power. They lead by serving. That style of leadership energizes them.

Jim from the Midwest illustrates this view. "In my

chancery experience," he said, "one of the things that I found out quickly, because I dealt with complaints, was that a lot of people have been away from the Church because a priest or a religious sister in the past did something to them and it has stuck in their minds. Starting my first pastorate, I was determined and I am still determined to not be that type of agent to somebody else. I am determined to try to be helpful and compassionate to them."

Fred, a Western chancery official, said, "So often what I've been exposed to are the horror stories, the things that people have been de-energized and turned off with and angered by in the Church. And for me, being full of life is to turn that around to provide them a really good experience."

Eric, 43, a Southern pastor, said, "I know in myself that when it comes to dealing with controversy, often it seems to be a choice between principles or people. I'll try to go for both. I won't go just for principle. Again, I've learned over the years that there is very little worth driving someone out of the Church over. Very little."

Bill from the West looks to the Catholics who come to church only on Christmas and Easter: "For years I have heard priests just berate people who only came to church on Christmas and Easter. And what I've adopted now is what I heard a priest say a long time ago, 'Thank you for coming. All of you who don't regularly come here, know how less a Church we are without you. We need you. And how much better, how much easier the load of the whole Church would be, if all of you participated.'"

Dick from the South said, "Looking back on my life now, I realize that another thing that has given me life is a desire not only to be proud of the talents God has given me, but to realize He has given them to me to put them into service."

The need to be kind and the sense of service that priests feel are expressed in the way they work to empower and animate the people they serve. Phil from the Midwest talked about the themes or coats of arms for his pastorates. The theme for the first pastorate was "Let my people go!"; the theme for the second was, "Remember, they were here first. And they are going to be here a long time after you go!"

Jack from the Midwest said,

> Part of the challenge of this era in history is calling people to their own rightful ministry and their rightful ownership of their part of the Gospel. I love to see people blossom. Empowerment is telling people that they have the right and the gift. Enablement is giving them the skills to realize it. Nothing makes me happier than when someone discovers that, 'Gee, I can do this. I can get involved in this ministry. I can make this presentation. I can lead a group.' The Lord is there. They have the experience of the Lord empowering them. They get excited and to me that is satisfying.

Pat from the West works with Spanish-speaking immigrants. He talked about how life-giving it was to watch them grow and become a part of the community and the Church. He said it is life-giving to observe "ordinary working-people start to realize that they have power and they have a lot of potential."

Fred from the West described his view of the priesthood: "I don't want the people to just focus on me so that when I leave, everything falls apart. But when we can build and I can see a community that is built authentically by their being in touch with each other and the lives they live, to me that is very life-giving."

Don from the Midwest talked about beginning his pastorate and doing a lot of listening, so he could join the parish before leading it. He talked about spiritual renewal emerging as a theme and priority of the parish. Talking about the staff he said: "We have organized to try to say, 'What helps you come alive? What can this parish do to help you live more deeply?'"

Priests cannot be understood apart from the support they receive from the people they serve. While the priests in our study have held an amazingly broad range of jobs, they talk most about their life in parishes and their contact with people. They see people who "keep the faith," even during life's most difficult moments, and it gives meaning to their own lives as priests. That, in turn, makes priests more sensitive to people's lives, more willing to listen, more compassionate, more empowering. And that in turn makes them better priests who are better able to serve the people of God. It's a circle of giving life.

Part Two

How Do You Deal With the Controversies Facing the Church Today?

J im, a Midwestern priest, related an incident that took place on an elevator: "I was visiting a hospital and I got on an elevator. There was a lady and her little boy, and they were kind of apart, but he definitely wasn't in the way. I come on with my collar and I go to the other corner and she grabbed her little boy and kind of clutched him to her. Boy, that is when the whole thing hit me. She didn't even know me. I am a pretty good person. I am a good person. And, ooh, that really hurt, that hurt."

Given all the publicity about priest pedophilia cases, it would have been impossible to talk to a group of priests and not address the issue. But rather than focus solely on pedophilia, we asked more vaguely about "the controversies" facing the Church in order to see what other issues would surface, such as morale problems, women's issues, and so on.

The priests in this study are, as we will see shortly, and as Jim's story indicates, concerned about the impact of pedophilia cases on the Church and the priesthood. But pedophilia did not top the list of controversies that concern these men. They were far more likely to talk about the growing gap they see between Church leadership on one side and the clergy and laity on the other. Many of the pastors expressed gratitude that they could involve themselves in parish life and distance themselves somewhat from some of the institutional issues of the Church. John, a Western pastor, said, "I think people experience Church and affirm Church at the local level."

Eric, a Southern priest, said, "I don't pay a whole lot of attention to the larger hierarchical Church controversies, to be honest with you. I am much more centered on the local church level. I am, however, very much involved in the bigger social issues of racism and violence and that kind of stuff. "

Art, a Southern priest, put it this way: "Yes, there are theological issues that are going to be discussed for a while...the issue of women priests, celibacy, and things like that, but the issues of priesthood for me are the issues of the daily living out of the Church, which is by and large the people right here along with us."

Joe, a Western priest, sees a fearful Church.

> As I look at the Church today I think that we have a Church that is working out of, at least in part, a model of fear. We have a fearful Church. I think leaders are fearful. It's like we have to mouthe the party line and we are afraid to question whether what we are doing is the best way. We can't just bring it out on the table and say, 'I think this is a bunch of crap.' We are afraid to do that. Bishops are afraid. I think that those in positions of leadership are afraid of what the

Vatican is going to say. So I think we do have an atmosphere of fear which is the worst possible way to live. And I think that we have to make a decision personally that we are not going to live out of fear. The right wing is everywhere. They are writing letters to Rome. The Vatican is responding to the American scene because of that. I think that we have to be careful not to get caught up in being fearful.

Peter from the South doesn't seem to be caught up in being fearful. He talks about his reactions to controversy as ranging from acceptance to proactively opposing and speaking up. A lot depends on whether he is convinced it is a worthwhile issue or that something that is being done is unfair or unjust, and whether his speaking up can make a difference. "It is somewhat like the serenity prayer, knowing what you can change and what you can't change," he said. "Sometimes it is a matter of doing everything that I can, doing the best I can, and then releasing it and letting it go. If an issue comes up, I will speak my piece and then step back and let somebody else speak their piece and then let somebody else do their thing. When it has been done, we move on, we keep going. But I also find that if an issue hasn't been resolved properly, it's going to come back again until it gets resolved properly."

A number of the priests raised the issue of dealing with controversial teachings. For Fred , a Western priest, it's a matter of understanding that the Church's teaching is not a judgment, even though many people interpret it that way. He said it is liberating for him to be able to tell people the teaching is not a judgment. He sees himself as "a docent for life. To be able to give people the skills to interpret what is going on so that they can deal with it in their consciences and not be bothered by it."

Rick, a Western tribunal official, said that working with people who are mature in their faith helps him deal with controversies: "They have a sense of conscience and are not always battling the Church because the Church did not give them permission to do this or that. For those who are not mature in their faith, I want to say, 'Stop blaming the Church and stop being a child and just grow up.'"

For Rick, the important thing is connecting people's lives and the Gospels. "I find that I am not in an easy position of saying I'm really comfortable with everything that we do in the Church or teach, but yet I find myself more alive. I don't want to leave. There is tension. There is conflict. There is vitality. There is joy. There is resolution."

George from the East said he is hurt by the priest-bashing that he occasionally experiences. Moreover, he does not like being a target of wider Church issues. For example, if he happens to use some non-inclusive language, "somebody is usually waiting out there for me, ready to jump all over me, as if I am a chauvinistic pig or whatever. That hurts. I would be comfortable with ordained women and having married clergy. But the Church is very clear on its position on that and there is nothing that I can do about it. So, don't hit me. Allow me to function as who I am and don't be out to jump me or put me down or put me off to the side somewhere."

Rick experiences tension between the people and the law. "When people call up now in the tribunal and they are angry at me and question why they have to go through this whole thing, I sometimes think, you are right. You are right to feel this way. You are entitled to feel this way. You are angry. I acknowledge that. I can't do anything about it aside from hearing it. I have no authority to resolve this, and I don't find that the institutional Church, whether it's the Pope, the Roman Curia, or the hierarchy, possesses the compassion and wisdom that I would expect."

Comments like these are particularly surprising because they come from what is admittedly a fairly "Establishment" group of priests; all were nominated as examples of "effective" and "respected" priests by diocesan officials, including bishops. But these priests are not simply rebels out and about in private practice; they reveal a common pattern of people-centered, pastoral concern.

What came out in this discussion of the controversies was neither a disdain for nor a deference to the institutional dimensions of the Church, but rather a healthy distance. Gene, from the Midwest, summed it up: "I think you have to come to grips with where you stand with the Church as institution and life in general. And I don't know if it's healthy distance or maybe just acceptance of the humanity of it all."

These men love the Church. But they are critical lovers because they want the Church to be all that it can be. And they are loving critics because they are men of the Church. But for them, Church means more than institution. "I love the Church," said one pastor. "It's not perfect and once I realized that, I was comfortable."

Bob from the Midwest said,

> I remember reading an essay by Chesterton about commitment and love. Chesterton said, 'If you love the Church or anything for a reason, and that reason is no longer there, your love is no

> longer going to be there. But if you just decide
> I am going to love it, that is it. It's kind of a risky
> bet. I will love the Church. There is a kind of
> real freedom in that. Whatever happens in the
> Church, I can choose the way to respond.

"What helps me," said Ken, a Southern priest, "is that I am quite aware of my own sinfulness and, because of that, I can accept it in the broader Church. I tend to be more grateful to the Church than I am angry with it. But sometimes, I can get rather depressed."

Gary, a Midwestern priest, said, "The future of the Church may look very unsettled and dark at this point in history for some people. But I think that if we wrap our sense of peace and happiness into an institution, then we take on that darkness and cloudiness or unsettledness into ourselves. Our sense of happiness and peace has to come from within."

Don, a Midwestern priest, said, "It's life-giving to me to be part of the wider Church and it's very important to me to let the screwy stuff of the Church go. Because there is a lot of stuff that I can't control. There is a lot of goofiness in the Church. And it will always be that way. To let go of a lot of that is a gift. To have the Church, to have the good things that come with the Church, but to let go of some of the monkey business."

Gary said, "We need to be able to overlook the goofiness, and live with the unanswered, the unsettled, and the less than perfect in the Church and in other people, too. Maybe most importantly, I need to be able to live with that in myself and be able to say, 'Yeah, this is stupid and it doesn't make any sense and I wish it weren't this way. But here it is, so where are we going to find God's grace in this?'"

Not taking the Church too seriously helps John from the West. "The Church is not the be all and end all," he said. "Maybe the kingdom is or something else out there is, but the Church isn't the whole schmear."

"The Church is not the be all and end all" is another way of saying that the Church is not the end but the means. What came across in all the focus groups is that these men are into the renewal agenda for the Church expressed in the Second Vatican Council. An underlying assumption in most of the comments about the Church is that the Church is not for itself, the Church is for the mission given it by Christ. The Church is for serving the movement or reign of God in this world.

A Western priest, formerly an associate pastor and now working in the chancery, put it this way: "If I can see the community focus on Christ..and what the coming Kingdom is supposed to be about, and how we are gifted with the Spirit now to begin that work, those are the things that really give me life."

Pedophilia

The reaction of these effective priests to the pedophilia issue is mixed. On the one hand, they see it having a negative impact on the Church and the image of the priesthood. Rick, for example, said there are times when being a priest is something you don't want to call attention to. Mark, an Eastern priest, said, "I have to say I've been very circumspect whenever I'm around teens. Fifteen, twenty years ago you would not have hesitated in taking a group of teens out to the creek. Now I just don't do that. We are living in a different age."

Rick said the parish's credibility in the community helped him deal with the scandals. "You can hold your head high because we were engaged in the community. If we weren't, then I would feel like, 'Oh God.'"

Frank, a Southern priest, spoke of the tension of being advised to be very careful about touching children, and being in an African-American community where touching and holding is affirming and a way of life. You are advised to become "a cold monolith on the playground."

On the other hand, priests see some positive outcomes of the pedophilia scandals. For one thing it highlights the importance of the individual priest witnessing to and representing the priesthood. Some of the priests felt a stigma when they represented "Priesthood" to people who did not know them, but felt no problem when people knew them. Don from the Midwest said, "Sometimes when I am in an anonymous place with a collar on, I feel people projecting all kinds of stuff onto me. But in the parish I feel very little of it. It doesn't get in my way and it doesn't limit my ministry much."

"The scandals hurt," said Bob from the Midwest. "I wouldn't be human if they didn't. But somehow I want to say I can handle that. I can process that and move beyond that. I can make a statement about what it means to be a healthy priest in the larger society."

Don said that while he is well aware of the pedophilia situation, "It doesn't stop me from tickling the kids once in a while. I think we are fine if we just stay grounded in ourselves, we don't have to stop that."

Walt from the Midwest said, "I think people receive us as we are. And so I don't feel threatened today by the scandals. I just hope that the goodness that is out there and the sincerity can overshadow that and give people a chance to recognize us as who we are."

What seemed clear is that these priests hoped to be perceived and judged as individuals rather than as a group. There seems to be a shift here. Thirty years ago "the priesthood" was able to "carry" or give credibility to individual priests. Today, because of the scandals, individual priests are "carrying" or giving credibility to "the priesthood."

These priests saw the situation in the Church as a "graced moment" because the scandals have called forth an honesty and an end of denial from Church leaders and has brought forth a deep compassion for the victims. And perhaps, they say, it will help bring about the end of clericalism. A Southern priest said, "Maybe this is good because it may be the beginning of the death knell of clericalism."

An Eastern pastor talked about an adult education series his parish ran on sexual abuse in the Church. It was around the time that Cardinal Bernardin was accused so there was a lot of interest. "I think one of the ways you deal with it is to talk about it," he said. "The worst thing is not to talk about it or pretend it doesn't exist. I think the secrecy has been really devastating. To have a healthy discussion about it with a group of normal people is one really helpful way of dealing with it."

George, another Eastern priest, said:

> Everybody is trying to learn how to deal with this reality. What do you do? How do you respond? I think the blessing of all this has been oddly, or maybe, ironically, that we've finally been responding to the victims in a sensitive way, which was a terrible blind spot for the institution. That

will probably be most helpful for future victims
and past victims who aren't speaking out. I think
it has created a kind of climate where people
know they will be responded to effectively.

Frank sees it as an invitation to conversion for the
Church: "This is part of the emptying out that we have to
do of the sin that is within us."

Effective priests don't shy away from controversy,
whether it involves scandal or institutional divisions. They
feel capable of handling controversy when they turn to their
most effective resources — the life-giving power of the Gospel, the people they know and serve, their own sense of
mission, and their trust that somehow God's Grace is in all
of this.

How Do You See Your Role As a Man in American Society?

B ill, a Western priest, recently went to the ordination of a Vietnamese seminarian. "The banner over his head at the reception at the ordination party was all in Vietnamese. I asked somebody, 'What does that mean?' Someone translated it. It said, 'He is no longer a man.'"

Bill was taken aback by the banner, and most of the priests in this study would be as well. Their candid discussions at our focus groups make it quite clear that priests are, in fact, men. Much of the discussion of the priesthood, both inside and outside the Church, treats priests as though they were a third gender, neither male nor female. These priests know better; they know that they are men.

Men in America are identified primarily in terms of their work, and these men feel they get respect for their work. George from the East is pastor of a parish consisting of college-educated, professional-level members. "I feel very much a peer to the people in that community and they communicate that to me," he said. "They expect certain things from me in terms of leadership. I get an enormous amount of respect from the people that I work with."

George continued, "One of the things that I pick up from people is that they know the difference between office and competence. Some of the young guys just assume that because they have an office, they have some rights. Lay people know the difference between somebody who makes that assumption and somebody who produces and is competent. So I find the professional respect that we get from people is based on our competence and our performance, and not on our office."

The pride of these priests in their competence at their jobs is tied in with their intellectual training. Tim from the West said, "One of the best pieces of advice that somebody gave me when I was in the seminary was, 'Nobody can take away your competency.'" Another priest said, "I like to think we are professional in what we do."

Mark, a pastor and former diocesan official, said,

> People see priesthood as something very mysterious. They may not understand it, and they may not agree with celibacy, but I find people have tremendous respect for the priesthood. And I don't feel at all insecure about what I'm doing, or who I am as a result. I don't feel my profession is certainly any less adequate than a doctor. I think the astute Catholics today realize that being a priest today is very challenging, and because of that I find they are more empathetic. That's my experience. They know we've got a tough job, just dealing with a lot of the negativity, and also with the great challenges that face the Church today. If they see a priest who's really trying to hang in there and really trying to do the best he

can, they have tremendous respect for him.

Being a man in American society involves relationships. As we saw earlier, for these men being celibate is not incompatible with having intimate relationships. Some priests see their celibacy as giving them freedom for intimacy. Jeff, an Eastern priest, sees his priesthood as giving him freedom as a man to do a variety of things:

> There's still a tension that you don't have children, that you are not married, and there are a lot of periods of loneliness by virtue of that, and I live alone. But there's still freedom. And I think that freedom also gives us the opportunity for intimacy that none of my own brothers experience. In the same way, I think of the different boards that I sit on and the committees that we all work on with laymen. They respect the intimacies that we share with a variety of people. These intimacies impact my vision and what I bring to preaching, to ministry, and to my job. I think in some ways we are able to glean a deeper level of God's activity than some other men really are able to glean. I think it's a freedom that allows for a deeper intimacy with how God's plan really does unfold. To me that's a blessing.

Not that celibacy is not difficult. Rick, a Western priest, described two lessons he learned as a young priest about sex and the priesthood: "Two wizened pastors, on separate occasions, mentioned something to me and I thought it was very freeing. It didn't solve the struggle, but it's just freeing. One told a story of how your sexual urges never leave you. In his own joking way he said 'They don't leave you even when you are old like me.' And another old pastor said, 'Yeah, and priests fall in love several times.' And it wasn't a big deal. It was information from a perspective that I appreciated. It was also very freeing. It is still a struggle, but at least I know that this is not just something that's new with my generation. It's part of the package."

Mike from the Midwest talked about a difficult time in his priesthood when he discovered that he had strong feelings for a woman in the parish. "I'm 38 years old," he said. "I don't need this. God, I don't need these feelings. I am secure in my priesthood. She is secure in her marriage. I never dated in high school. I played sports. I struggled with school. I had to study hard to get the grades. I worked in a gas station to enable myself to go to a Catholic school and I never took time to date. Here I am 38 years of age and I'm a happy priest and here I have feelings for this woman. I had to deal with that. That was difficult."

Jack from the Midwest said his perspective changed when someone suggested that he look at celibacy as a gift from the Lord. "That was a change of reference for me," he said. "I used to think of celibacy as my gift to the Lord. This is what I was giving the Lord. A friend said, 'Think of celibacy as what the Lord has given you, not what you are going to give the Lord.' And I began to think about that and pray over that. And it changed. Celibacy was never a big problem or issue for me, but when I began to ask for the gift of celibacy, it seemed like I received the freedom that it brings to love. It seemed that there was more life and vitality out of that. And it seems like a gift, not a burden. It's what I am receiving rather than what I am giving."

These respected priests see their role as counter-cultural. Fred noted that he had heard at a conference that the role of priest is so counter to the role of the male in our society. "We spend a lot of time with women. We can, by and large, hold up in a conversation which the women have among themselves in the sense that we can talk about feelings, we can be sensitive in public, we can be compassionate and caring. Yet, at the same time, we can divest ourselves of that and be the macho or be the man or whatever the society role is. Or, we don't need to do that. I mean there is that freedom of just being who you are and rising up against it. There is almost fun in tweaking the societal expectation of what a man is by being a priest."

Bob, a Midwestern priest, also sees priests as countercultural.

> We live in a society that really discourages reflection. We have beer commercials that say, 'Why ask why?' We have commercials that depict a bunch of guys around a campfire drinking beer, frying fish, saying 'It doesn't get any better than this.' We have commercials that say, 'You are on your way to the top and you've always known just who you are.' We all know that that is all bull. I think we live in a society that really discourages reflection on life. When people feel pain, it tells them to take two little yellow pills and it's gone. I think there is a real danger that we will become technological giants and spiritual infants; that we will know everything about how but nothing about why. I think that we priests have a tremendous amount to offer society in terms of teaching, leading others to reflect on their own lives, and being available for them at those times when they do need some reflection. I think we are a hidden jewel.

Bill, a Western priest, said priests need to be counter cultural regarding consumerism. "One of the other dangers that we all know is materialism. We have got priests trying to get the most toys. You know, the latest electronic rectory or the almighty computer that we worship. Some are getting addicted to things or alcohol because of loneliness or the dysfunctionality."

John from the West put it this way:

> We are talking about being a model of the healthy man, but not in terms of society's definition of masculinity, which defines it in terms of how much money you make. Our urban societies are falling apart because we have set up these definitions of what it means to be a man. I see kids who only know how to relate or touch another through aggression. I think we have a strong responsibility to image or be a sign of testosterone that is not directed towards violence. I think it's imperative that we have a healthy image, a sign of hope for what to do with love. Nobody is out there teaching people how to be tender. Sexuality has been separated from love. Sex is pleasure or its aggression or it's dysfunction.

Tim from the West feels very comfortable with himself as a man: "I don't feel I have to prove anything to anybody. I find it very freeing being a male. I can be myself. I can support women. I don't feel women are a threat. They are friends. I don't have to be jealous of fellow priests for their talents because I feel I have a certain amount of talents — enough for me to work on. If I can be that kind of person, that is a good male role model."

Dick, an Eastern priest, talked about the experience of building a bond with other men through a history-sharing process in a parish renewal program. "We sit around the table and we share histories. That creates a lot of bonds among men in our parish...it's probably the greatest cement. I see myself as very much a part of that. I see myself relating to these men in a very brotherly way, as peers."

One Western priest reads Sam Keen and other authors who write about what it means to be a man. Neil, an Eastern priest said, "Maybe at times I don't know my maleness enough, so I'm actually considering a retreat experience later on this year that's going to focus on that. I feel I need to do it because I feel sometimes that I can relate and interact and hang out with other men and have a couple of beers and all that, but sometimes I feel uncomfortable with that."

Bill from the West said, "I have to be a life-giving, loving person. That means to be honest with who I am. Being life-giving and loving doesn't mean I have to jump into the sack with everybody as society might say. But, rather, wherever I encounter people, I try to give life to that encounter, to bring love to that encounter."

There's another aspect of the way that priests view themselves as men in society; some priests miss an often ignored role of manhood — fatherhood. Rick says: "I would like to have children, or something generative, responsible, or be a mentor for somebody else at this point in my life. I think about the next generation, and those kinds of experiences that are common to all men and women are important."

Jeff, an Eastern priest who is one of nine children, talked about the way he responds when people ask him,

"How can you be a priest? Don't you have any desire to be married?"

> I'm not sure personally because I really do feel fulfilled and feel I really enjoy intimacy with people. I don't feel a major, compelling force to be married. But I always say that if there is one regret that I have, it is the fact that I will never have any children. And that for me is more of a tension than the fact of never actually being married. You know, just what would it be like? But, you know, I think I share enough with my own nieces and nephews and some other families. An example: Charlie, another staff person, called me the other night about five o'clock with a question and our secretary said, 'Well, he's up-stairs playing hide and seek.' Now, our office closes at 4:30, and this Charlie had thought that literally I just did not want to answer the phone. Well, now, at five o'clock my secretary's grand-son, who is two years old, was in the office build-ing and I was playing hide and seek with a two-year-old. That's because it's life-giving. You know, just to share in some of that intimacy and just the natural joy of families. That's where I came from, and that's why I hope to continue sharing it.

But these priests still sometimes feel tension in an all male clergy. George from the East described tensions with women:

> I feel a lot of pressure as a male cleric trying to relate to equally competent women who feel that they don't have a role or that they are not

recognized and acknowledged. That creates a lot
of tension in my parish community. They feel
they don't get a fair shake in the whole question
of ordination of women. And I find that the gaffs
and the mistakes that I make usually have to do
with the fact that I'm not as sensitive to the role
of women. I feel unsure. I instintively understand male company but I don't understand female company.

These respected priests are also aware of tensions between gay and straight priests. One priest wondered about
the impact of a "largely gay priesthood," ministering to a
largely straight laity. Other priests agreed that those tensions
exist, although none either challenged or confirmed the
characterization of the priesthood as "largely gay."

One interesting aspect of priests' feelings about their
role as men in American society involves their attitudes
toward priestly garb. A surprising amount of discussion
focused on when, where, and why priests wear clerical garb.
Tim, a Western priest, said, "I am the same person whether
I am in a collar or out of a collar. I try to be consistently
the same."

Fred, another Western priest, offers this appraisal:

I live with this retired priest and he is always
giving me a bad time about how many times I'll
change clothes during the day — 'Is that another
outfit?' But if I am shifting gears, I change clothes
according to what I am going into. If I'm not
doing a priestly thing, I don't want the clerical
clothes on. If I go to the gym, I change clothes.
When I put on a chasuble to celebrate the Eucha-

rist, that is the acceptance of that role. But I'm not only a set of roles.

When I was working in our old office downtown, we would always go for a walk in the park after lunch and it was really difficult when one of our priests was in a trial for clergy abuse. You might as well be walking around naked. There was a gay rights protest group one day, and we wanted to get past them, we just didn't want to be caught up at all in that. Now we are in a new office, we have lockers, and I am looking forward to being able to change my clothes and go for a walk on my lunch hour. I can relax when I go out and walk rather than be hit up for change.

An Eastern priest refuses to wear black when he travels:

It's just one of those times where you finally have some quiet time to yourself. If I'm on an airplane, I just want to read. It's a couple of hours that you really can just kind of catch up on pleasant reading or sometimes even read a report that you didn't get a chance to focus on. It's more personal time when I really don't choose to get involved in somebody else's issues at that point, and I need that time.

But, Al from the East always wears his collar on planes because it "gives you all sorts of opportunities."
Gene, a Midwestern priest, said,

I live at the rectory on the east side of the street and I work at the Catholic Center on the west side of the street. I cross a very busy street every day. Of course, you cross at the light most of the time, and cars are standing there and I'm walking across with my collar on going to the office. Lots of times I think, 'I wonder what they are thinking? A priest crossing!' And I must admit there are times when I suspect that those thoughts aren't positive thoughts. What is going through their minds?

Now, on the other hand, when it's a setting where I feel like I have the chance to identify myself, I have the chance to create the impression in their mind of who I am. If I stand in front of a group to give a talk and they have never met me before, I have the chance to let them walk out of the building with some understanding of who Gene, the priest, is. I feel comfortable in those settings. So, when I feel that I've got a chance to mold the impression, I am at home.

Bob from the Midwest wears clerical garb every day: "I want to say that this is who I am and I am going to dress this way. It's a freeing thing. The scandals hurt but somehow I want to say I can handle that and move beyond that. I can make a statement about what it means to be a priest that is healthy in the larger society."

It is clear that when these men talk about clerical garb, they do not see it as an end in itself or as giving them their identity. Rather they wear it or not based upon how it serves the ministry or identifies them with the larger mission of the Church.

These particular priests are comfortable with their role as men in American society. They do not stop being men once they are ordained. They enjoy being good at what they do. They see their manhood as a form of ministry and a way to be counter-cultural.

What Advice Would You Give to Seminary Personnel Today?

The seminary played an important role in shaping the priests in this study. They expressed a mixed reaction to their own formation for priesthood and a highly, though not completely, critical view of today's seminarians. They are concerned about today's seminaries which are training a new generation of priests.

Speaking of their own experiences on the positive side, a number of priests praised the fine academic background that the seminary provided. Roy, a Southern priest, was grateful to the seminary for "teaching me to think" and for giving him "an excellent academic approach to things." Dick, a Southern priest, said, "I can truthfully say that a lot of what I am as a priest is due to a wholesome, happy and good seminary training." What made it good, he said, was integration — "our academic formation was linked together with our spiritual formation."

Good modeling by priests was also significant to these men when they were seminarians. Gary from the Midwest is grateful for the people in the seminary who had a good sense of balance and perspective "about what's important in life and what's not important, what is a catastrophe and what isn't a catastrophe." Fred from the West talked about the seminary as his first exposure to really competent priests. The rector in particular was a model for him. Fred described him as "an eloquent speaker, his own person, not just a good institutional person. He allowed a lot of creativity and life to happen, allowed a lot of humor. It was like a buffet of life was spread out."

Dick remembered a significant experience as a novice: "One of our jobs was to take care of the bedridden monks as they died. This was difficult but wise, because as we began, we were in touch with the end. We became attached to them and heard their stories and realized that someday we'd be doing the same thing, telling our stories to some young monk."

Gary said, "I'm grateful to the people I encountered in the seminary who gave me a love for the Church...that you are here to be part of a larger project than your own little thing...and a belief that the Church is a force for good and even miracles in the world." One priest mentioned that the Benedictines taught him the beauty of the liturgy and the beauty of prayer; he saw this as a real contribution to him and to the diocese.

Many of the priests cited valuable friendships as a positive experience of seminary formation. John from the West remembered the significance of an institute that took place prior to leaving the seminary and starting his first assignment; it dealt with sexuality, relationships, moving into a new system, living in rectories, and so on. "I found it invaluable," he said, "to have some place to process stuff that was happening to us in that period of change in moving out of the seminary. It was also a process whereby guys who had lived together for years were able to bring closure on some angers and hates and fears and things that had happened over the years."

John mentioned the Vietnam War period as extremely formative in that "there was a lot of energy and decision towards a radical conviction for the Gospel that really forced people to get involved." Roy thought studying in Canada helped him get a more pluralistic approach to theology, culture, worship, and different types of spirituality.

Peter from the South told a colorful story to indicate what the seminary taught him: "A little sparrow delayed a little too long in leaving the north and flying south to get out of the cold weather. And the cold front came through and as he is flying, his wings begin to ice up and he falls to the ground and he lies there covered with ice and gets ready to die. As he is laying there, a cow walks by and drops a cow pie on top of him. And, of course, the cow manure is very warm. It melts the ice. It warms him up. He begins to feel great and he starts to sing. And as he starts chirping away, a cat passing by hears him and grabs him, pulls him out of the manure and eats him.

"There are three morals to the story and that is what I learned from the seminary. First of all, everybody who craps on you is not your enemy. Secondly, when you are in crap up to your nose, don't sing about it. And thirdly, not everybody who rescues you from crap is your friend."

On the negative side, these priests criticized the lack of honesty and trust when they were in the seminary as contributing to a somewhat repressive environment. Some said that sexuality was not something about which you could be really honest in the seminary, and one priest observed that the "celibacy talks never rang true."

Tim from the West said, "My experience in the seminary was that it's not a place of holiness. Seminary was not a place where people could be honest and talk about real issues of peoples' lives without fear. There was little formation that went on. If I hadn't had the grace of God and the Holy Spirit to continue to develop some on my own, it just would not have happened."

Roy remembered that one's inadequacies were the focus of his seminary days. "Priesthood is an unlearning," he said, "because we were always seen as less than adequate when we were in the seminary. We were here, but they wanted us to be over there. So they had to mold and maneuver and manipulate and destroy what was here to bring it over there. And I think that affected our self esteem and the way we moved into our ministry. God never sees me as anything less than wonderful."

Concerns about Seminarians and Newly Ordained

These effective priests are concerned about today's seminarians and newly ordained — "scary" was a word they used a number of times to describe the situation; one priest said the seminary in his diocese needed an exorcism.

One priest in his forties recalled that when he was in the seminary, "We were the liberals. When we got out, the older priests tended to be more conservative. Now it's just the opposite. The ones who are the conservative ones are the younger guys coming out and we are the flaming liberals still. And I find that a very strange position to be in."

But more than politics or middle-aged grousing is involved here. These priests see, in some new priests, values and lifestyles at odds with much of what gives them life. The nature, depth, and emotion of their comments indicate that something much more than middle-aged grousing is involved. Some of what they see happening today is at odds with their hard-earned experience.

Many see a return to clericalism and a style of ministry that "Lords it over people." They see many as being more into a kingly priesthood than a servant priesthood. Bill from the West is concerned about his two associates: "I've never experienced the royal priesthood more in my life than in these young men. It's like: 'I am the priest, I say it and that should be it. Now God has given me this power in ordination and I am now going to make all you people jump through hoops.' That is very scary!"

Neil, an Eastern priest, said, "They think now that 'Father knows best', and it is such a put-down on people. I understand that they need people to be ordained, but it's frightening." Jim from the West sees clericalism as symptomatic of some deeper issues. "Clericalism is one way to not deal with who I am. I put the mask on. That is the real danger with this clericalism. It's a dramatic return to superficiality." Mark from the East sees the underlying problem as an inadequate concept or vision of Church: "They see the Church as a pyramid and because I'm newly ordained, I'm at the top of the pyramid and you as a lay person are way down here."

George, an Eastern priest, said, "In Scripture, the Lord sent the disciples out two by two, and said, 'Go and eat with the people before you teach them,' and that's so true. They think they can teach the people without living with them and eating with them."

These respected priests worry about whether the Church is admitting unhealthy men into the priesthood. One priest said, "We're not getting what I would consider healthy individuals." Similarly, a Midwestern priest warned against co-dependency:

> We are experiencing co-dependency. I think the Church sometimes is probably cooperating in this. We develop a co-dependent relationship between the Church or diocese and the individual. They expect the Church to take care of them. We should look into some of those things in order that they don't walk into priesthood with a dependency that isn't healthy.

Effective priests worry that often the seminarians lose themselves in a role and don't honestly deal with who they are. It's as if they try to cover over themselves and their sexuality with a role, the collar, the cassock, and/or ritual. Bill from the West talked about priests retreating into the sanctuary behind a clerical wall — "I'm finding the altar rail is up again."

The priests in this study are concerned about seminarians and the newly ordained's capacity for service and magnanimous living. Jack from the Midwest points out that "we have certainly gotten the message across to the seminarians that they have to take care of themselves." But, he wonders and worries how they are going to adapt to some of the inevitable demands that will be put upon them as pastors. "Life is not quite as neat and orderly as they are demanding it to be," he said. "Yes, you do need to protect yourself. But, there also has to be some flexibility and some willingness to do some things you don't choose for yourself."

In the context of talking about seminarians Gary mentioned something that he learned from his family. He said it almost as a wish that all seminarians could learn the same thing: "I'm one of twelve children. In a family that size you get a sense that the world does not turn on its axis according to your schedule, and the sun doesn't rise and set on your head."

These men are also concerned that some newly ordained seem to have all the answers and have a tough time listening. They question their capacity and willingness to work with people. Mark from the East commended seminarians for their intelligence and knowledge of theology, law, history, and liturgy, but said, "They've forgotten what the virtue of humility is . . . to be sensitive, to be listeners."

Bill from the West is concerned that seminarians are threatened by lay people and don't see them as co-workers. He said they say, for example, "I am the expert liturgist, so don't tell me what you have been doing here for the last 20 years. This is not what Hoyle says in the liturgy book."

Carl from the East complained that "My brothers in the clergy are my biggest pain"; he said many of the newly ordained are "anti-people, anti-women."

Gene from the Midwest made an interesting observation on relating to people and the Eucharist. He put it this way:

> I think love for the Eucharist flows out of love for the people. I think some are starting with a love for the Eucharist and don't have any notion of what it means to love God's people. That scares me because it tells me they are caught up in that external experience or they are caught up in an experience of God that doesn't have anything to do with their experience of other people. I think they really need to pay attention to that.

Effective priests also see a lack of flexibility and adaptability in today's seminarians. Roy saw "no flexibility at all in the young and newly ordained priests. I see a rigidity that is not only scary but is dangerous to them. It is unhealthy. It's a real murdering of the spirit because it's a rigidity that has no room for God and no room for God's people and that concerns me."

These priests are concerned that many newly ordained display a rigid, conservative thinking. They are concerned that these conservative seminarians are not being challenged in the seminary and are becoming entrenched. The result is that some seminarians leave the seminary with not much more theological insight than they entered with. They worry about future priests with a shallow theology and spirituality. Tim from the West said, "There is a radicalism within the seminary, but it's not radical to the Gospel and it isn't radical to prayer and it isn't radical to the movement of the Spirit. They are not being challenged."

Rick, who is involved in seminary work, questions the seminarians' initiative. "I don't know if the men have a great deal of initiative," he said. "I wonder if they have the initiative to continue on in their theological pursuit and deepen their understanding."

Effective priests see the need for future leaders in the Church and wonder whether the present seminarians will be up to it. For that task they need more than docility and obedience; those qualities might make for a tranquil seminary scene, but not for prophetic leadership. Many are concerned that the newly ordained seem to have set limits and qualifications for their ministry. They know where they will serve and where they won't. For example, John, a personnel board member, is concerned that none of the newly ordained want to go to parishes that are Hispanic, Vietnamese, or urban.

Two Midwestern priests used identical language to criticize newly ordained priests for having "blueprints" for their ministry. Jack said, "I worry sometimes that seminarians come out with their own blueprint of exactly where they are going to go and where they are not going to go with their life. And I think we'd be better served or they would be better served if it weren't quite so fixed." Bob said, "I have seen a lot of guys come out with blueprints and say if the bishop doesn't give me this assignment, then I am gone. And some have left. I know some who have left because the bishop has said, 'I'd like you to go here or there'. I don't want to portray them all as rigid, but I do think they could be more flexible."

Suggestions for Seminarians

One of the questions we asked the thirty-five priests assembled from the four regions of the country was: "What advice would you give to those involved in seminary administration and the formation of priests?" Their direct responses to that question are in the next section. However in their discussion of that question we were able to glean some advice and suggestions for seminarians.

Bill, a supervising pastor, tells his seminarian interns: "You have got to deal with who you are. You can't love anyone if you don't love yourself. I don't care what you are or what your interests are. Get in touch with them, be comfortable with them. Don't let them erupt in your life suddenly when you are 40 years old. Don't wait until you are 45 years old to realize you have a sexuality."

A number of priests suggested that the seminarian needs

to know who he is, what his strengths and limitations are, to do his "inner work." Gary, who has worked in vocations, added an interesting nuance by suggesting that there is a difference between doing your inner work in a healthy way and naval gazing. He suggests that a seminarian look at formation in this way: "Up to the internship (the first two years of theology) take the time to know who you are, what your strengths and gifts are, your weaknesses and shortcomings. Then after that, by God, come out of it. Begin to give. Begin to redirect your focus away from yourself so that you are able to meet the demands that will be reasonably expected of you."

Gene from the Midwest, who also was in vocations work, agrees: "You have got to immerse yourself in ministry before you can find what your balance is. Some are trying to work out their space before they have ever immersed themselves in ministry."

Peter from the South said, "First of all, be a seminarian. Don't try to be a priest. Don't try to be a deacon. Don't try to be a layman. Be a seminarian who is learning and growing. Secondly, be open to the fact that you don't have all the answers and that there are many different things that you can learn from other people around you, including the people that you don't respect or appreciate or with whom you disagree."

Art from the South gives some advice on learning: "There is a difference between learning and knowing. A professor once told me that if you can't talk to a second grader about what you learned in the seminary, you don't know it." Art advises the seminarian to let the knowledge "soak in and become a part of you."

Joe, a Western priest, said, "One thing that I would tell

seminarians when going out into their ministries would be to learn how to be respectful and nice to people. There are so many people who get hurt because priests are not nice to them."

These priests' advice to seminarians reflects the same themes that have run through the previous discussions: You have to be honest with yourself and with others. You need good role models and good personal relationships. You need to listen to people and to be good pastors. And you need to be in touch with God's grace in your life.

Advice to Seminary Personnel

The priests in our focus groups have been involved in many different ministries. All have had parish experience; some have been involved in vocation work and priest personnel work. They have varying knowledge and experience of today's seminary, but they all have experienced the newly ordained who are the products of today's seminaries. Those experiences and their own experience of what it takes to be an effective priest in today's Church and of what gives them life in the ministry evoked the following suggestions, made with some passion.

The recommendations that these priests have for seminaries today begin with a call to careful discernment. Joe, a former pastor and now a vicar for priests, said, "I think one of the major flaws that we have in seminaries at this point is the lack of discernment. Let me give you a case in point. There is a priest who went through the seminary recently who was an active alcoholic all through his seminary years, drank a good amount of hard liquor every night, and was ordained. Then, a year or two years into ministry he had to be sent away for alcohol rehabilitation. Now that is absolutely mind-blowing for me that a guy could get through five years of major seminary and that not be discovered. That is the fault of the diocese. That is the fault of the seminary. So, it seems to me that there is a lack of discernment with seminarians about their call and their response."

Joe suggested that seminaries be very careful about accepting newly converted persons into formation for priesthood and ordaining them only five years after their conversions to Catholicism.

Several priests emphasized the importance of a variety of role models in the seminary. Eric, a Southern priest, said, "I would hope that seminaries would continue to provide men and women who are great models of spirituality and pastoral life. Somehow, pastors should be connected with seminary training. That's important. Seminarians need a variety of perspectives on how to handle life. I didn't find the seminary prepared me well for pastoral life." An Eastern priest made the point, "Seminarians can't minister until they've been ministered to."

Tom from the West said that seminary professors have to be genuine. They also have to be true believers. "The people who are teaching at the seminary have a profound responsibility," he said. "They have to be authentic. Because for a lot of guys, that is going to be the beginning of their model of priesthood."

Rick, who teaches part-time at a Western seminary, admires the competence and goodness of the faculty.

> However, I do get concerned. Is this closed seminary system the best way to prepare men for priesthood? I am concerned that the forum of academic inquiry is too limited. They should have

men and women of other professions, other people in ministry, other faiths, so that they can have some kind of interchange and dialogue. I think it would give people a greater sense of security and confidence about their own theological expertise and their own commitment. My fear is that the closed system reinforces clericalism.

In a similar vein, a number of priests suggested that the seminary broaden its perspective. As John from the West put it: "The world is getting too small for us to look at it only from a European perspective." A broader perspective keeps the seminary from becoming a closed system and opens the seminarian to the pluralism that has always been a part of the tradition. Bill suggests that pluralism can also help in self acceptance: "It can help the men accept pluralism. It can help them accept the fact that there is more than one type of good person. The training we had was to make us all alike, even hiding our identity behind wearing the same clothes. It was tremendously freeing to realize that I could be different and still be good. It helped me in my acceptance of black people, of women, of ethnic differences, and ecumenism. That was very freeing. It still is."

The multicultural complexities of today's seminaries were apparent in at least two observations in this part of the discussion. Rick had some question about how people of different cultures understand what is taught in seminaries. For example, he said, "If you come from a culture that is patriarchal, how can you understand the vision of marriage as something mutual?" A West Coast pastor wondered why African Americans do not feel comfortable in Catholic seminaries while Vietnamese do.

Mark from the East noted that other professions such as medicine have a built-in apprenticeship or internship. "I've always been mystified," he said, "why as diocesan priests, six months or a year of mandatory supervised ministry has never been part of seminary formation!"

Bill from the West commended the seminary for the pastoral year in which the seminarian lives and works in a parish before he is ordained. He especially commended one program that insisted that the seminarian immediately get a core group of parishioners to meet with him regularly and give him honest feedback.

Art from the South, suggests that in some cases ordinary work experience in the marketplace might be of more value to some seminarians than ministry in a parish.

George, a former personnel director for priests, suggested that there be a kind of internship or learning period for the first three to five years after ordination. He believes that ought to be the Diocese's responsibility. He noted that probably all priests have had to learn on the job: "I was never assigned to a job that I knew how to do! Everything that I was assigned to, I had to learn on the job."

A persistent refrain in these men's suggestions was the wish that seminary staffs somehow be able to create an environment of trust and honesty where seminarians could talk about real-life issues. Tim from the West suggests that a system where the seminarians' professors are also their advisors, confessors, formation directors, and judges doesn't work: "It creates a dishonesty in the system."

Bill from the West suggests that two of the real-life issues that seminaries need to be honest about are sexuality and celibacy. "Don't deny that people are sexual beings," he said. "Don't treat people as if they are asexual. Don't simply say, 'Celibacy is a gift from God and we need say no more about it.'"

Rick noted that the seminary life still promotes a monastic type of spiritual life and routine that doesn't fit into diocesan priestly ministry. Bob from the Midwest also implied a suggestion for seminary staffs when he talked about his own spirituality and the emphasis in his own seminary formation on self perfection. "Now I've come to the realization in the ministry that the spiritual life is more about self surrender than self perfection." Carl from the East, a priest for thirty years, had a very simple suggestion: "Teach them how to pray!"

Two priests noted the tendency to try to include everything in the agenda of priestly formation. They both suggested that seminaries not try to do it all. What then should be the focus of seminary formation?

Don from the Midwest, a pastor who also worked in continuing education of clergy, thinks the seminary did a good job with his newly ordained associate. "He is a wonderful human being, levelheaded, and smart. The seminary gave him good academics, great scripture, some pastoral experience, and an opportunity for integration." According to Don, that is what the seminary ought to focus on. If you try to teach everything the person ought to know, "all of a sudden you have a 14-year program."

George, a pastor and former rector, acknowledged that it's a tough job to decide what priestly formation should be. If he had to design a system from scratch, he would put all of the practical and interpersonal skill training in internships and field experience with occasional seminars and workshops. "Let the seminary do what it does best, the academic piece. If the seminary doesn't do the academic piece, the priest will probably never go back and get the appropriate conceptual framework. A conceptual framework is really critical. If you don't have it, you simply can't do the job. If we don't have a theological point of view, we have nothing to add to the dialogue in society and the community."

Finally, Art, a priest born in Ireland, invoked the image of seminary formation as a golf course. "An American designed a golf course in Ireland. He designed it for the type of showers that you have over here which can be very heavy. He didn't design it for a soft persistent Irish rain, and that meant that the water that fell on the golf course wasn't doing any good. It was just running off and not nourishing the golf course." Art suggests that priestly formation is more like the soft Irish rain than the heavy downpour. "Perhaps we need to make sure our seminaries and our seminary programs are designed to take advantage of that, so that the rain doesn't just run off the surface."

The passion with which these respected priests talk about today's seminarians and newly ordained priests reflects the passion they feel about their own priesthood. It also reflects what one priest earlier described as the generative need to pass on what they have learned. What they have learned is how to be alive and effective, and they want seminaries to do as much as they possibly can to pass on that wisdom to the next generation of priests.

Conclusion

Grace Under Pressure

T he discussions of this study focused on what gives priests life. But in talking about that, these priests also talked about their fears. It should come as no surprise that they are afraid of things that would take away their sources of life. They feared: "being in a rut," "becoming bitter at life's disappointments," "dying after having lived only in a world of ideas and rituals," "saying something stupid to a dying person."

Fred from the West named a fear that brought nods of agreement from others in the focus group. "I think being a Circuit Rider Priest is the most scary thing." The image of the Circuit Rider comes up often in discussions of ways to deal with the priest shortage. The image pictures the priest traveling each weekend to a number of different congregations to preside at the Eucharist. This is already a reality in some parts of the country. The priests in this study would find that kind of life, devoid of on-going contact with people in a regular community, scary and very difficult, if not intolerable.

These priests are definitely aware of what it is that gives them life. Here is a summary of the many hours of discussion on that topic:

1. Risk-taking and Change. These men take risks

and look at life with enthusiasm. The images of jumping off cliffs, of living on the razor's edge, and of expanding the horizon reflect this very basic aspect of their personalities. Above all, they manage change well and even thrive on it.

2. Balance, Perspective, and Time. Not everyone who takes risks or thrives on change has a sense of balance. The combination of risk-taking and balance may be the most unusual aspect of these priests' make-up. They know what they can change and what they can't. They see their efforts as part of a larger scheme. They are intentional about their use of time and they make sure they get time to themselves. They don't take things too personally and they are able to laugh at themselves.

3. Authenticity. Effective priests place a premium on being authentic, on being honest, on not going through the motions. They want to tell it straight to their people, to themselves, and even to their superiors. Being authentic also means being accountable.

4. Multiple Intimacies. The priests in this study are not isolated and lonely men. Dr. John Mayer's earlier research, clinical interviews with more than 100 priests, found that the only happy priests were those who had developed intimate relationships, and that clearly is the case with these priests. They form close relationships within their families and build a strong supporting network of all kinds of friends — men, women, priests, ex-priests, religious sisters, lay people, Catholics, and non-Catholics. Some find support groups helpful. Some have formed special relationships with women.

5. The Significance of the Priesthood and the Mystery of the Call. The priests in this study are convinced that being a priest is a significant way to spend one's life. They are convinced that what they do is important to the Church and to society.

They are convinced of the power and importance of the Gospel for the world. They realize that their call to this mission is from God and is a mystery. They are still in awe of that and happy to be about God's agenda in the world.

6. God's Love. These men are sustained by the conviction that God is always with them and loves them and will take care of them. Underlying all the activities and pressures of their ministries, the controversies in the wider Church, the changes and difficulties in their personal lives, there is a God loving them. They depend on that relationship. They know they are "graced".

7. Relationship with Jesus and the Paschal Mystery. These priests are clear that their role model and mentor is Jesus Christ. "What would Jesus do?" is the question they ask themselves. Jesus' death and resurrection gives meaning and significance to the dying and rising that they experience in their own lives and the lives of the people. In the Paschal Mystery they move through death to life.

8. The Spiritual Life. These respected priests respond to God's love and Jesus Christ's challenges with their lives of ministry. But, they also respond with an active spiritual life involving prayer and scripture and liturgy. It all seems to flow together with these men. God loves them and challenges them. Aware of that, they respond in worship and prayer and ministry. God inspires, supports, and challenges them anew through worship and prayer and ministry.

9. Mystery of God's Activity in Life and Ministry. The belief that "there is something else going on here besides me" is at the heart of priesthood for these men. That something else is the activity and movement of God. These men see more than what meets the eye. They are in touch with the deeper reality of what God seems to be doing in the events and activities of daily life.

10. Drawing Life from the People. Effective priests draw life from the people they serve, and that in turn inspires them to serve those people better. It is a synergistic relationship. They draw inspiration from the example that lay people set in their own lives and they are awed by their role in people's lives at the key moments of birth, marriage, death, sickness, and suffering.

11. Listening. "Listen First" is the motto of these respected priests. It helps them serve. It helps them preach. In an analysis of recent surveys of a representative sampling of priests, Andrew Greeley remarked that there doesn't seem to be much listening going on in the Church. If that is so, these priests are an exception.

12. Service, Compassion, and Empowerment. Because they draw life from the people and because they have learned to listen to them, these priests are particularly sensitive to people's needs. Priesthood and their personal talents are not for them but for others. Priesthood for them is about serving, not being served. It is also about leading.

They see themselves as servant leaders, i.e., serving the people by calling and empowering them to serve others.

When the priests in this study must confront serious issues — the controversies facing the Catholic Church in the United States, their own role as men in American society, and the state of the next generation of priests — they draw on those things that give them life. This produces a consistent approach to all challenges.

They seem to be able to keep the Church in perspective. They see the Church not as an end in itself. The Church is the people of God on mission. The institutional aspects, the structures, and the laws are to serve the mission. Institutional issues that have little to do with the Gospel or the parish do not engage them. They acknowledge the imperfections and sinfulness in the Church. That is the reality. That is the Church they love and continue to challenge to be better.

In the controversies and scandals, they look for the grace. "Where are we going to find the grace in this?" They find God's grace for them personally in the challenge to speak the truth as they see it to bishops and the wider Church. They also find in the current situation God's invitation to make a positive personal statement by their actions of what it means to be a good priest in today's world.

They also recognize God's grace for the Church in the controversies and scandals. They see it as a call for the Church to repent. They believe that repentance will make the Church more responsive to victims, more honest, and less clerical.

These respected priests believe that their role as men in American society is to be counter-cultural. In a society that glorifies violence, competition, and materialism they see their role as offering an alternative way to be a man. They offer a life style that is reflective, compassionate, caring, and alert to the dangers of consumerism and materialism. They take delight in their competency without feeling the need to compete with others or prove themselves.

The passion with which these men voice their criticisms of today's seminarians and newly ordained priests reflects the passion with which they view their priesthood and their desire to pass on to the next generation what they know and how they perceive things. Their passion builds a link between priests who have no biological children and any father who has ever been desperate to pass on to his biological children his own knowledge and experience. They have experienced what gives life to them in the priesthood and they want to pass on that life.

It is significant that when these effective priests talk about the things that give them life and make recommendations to seminary personnel, they, in fact, reflect some of the wisdom found in Church documents on seminaries and the priesthood. For example, the U.S. Catholic bishops' statement, *Spiritual Formation in the Catholic Seminary*, states:

> The real growth in the spirituality of a person occurs in the realm of personal relationships, that is, the relationship of the person with the mystery of God in Jesus, with oneself, and with other persons. Thus, programs of formation are designed to serve the process of interpersonal relationships. The level and qualities of the fundamental relationships noted above are a gauge and an indicator of growth in one's spirituality.

The role that these relationships play in giving life to these priests dramatically illustrates the truth of the bishops' statement.

Similarly, Pope John Paul II endorsed the significance of human development in the formation process in his statement, *Pastores Dabo Vobis*. In particular, he said:

> The whole work of priestly formation would be deprived of its necessary foundation if it lacked a suitable human formation....We must not forget that the candidate himself is a necessary and irreplaceable agent in his own formation. All formation, priestly formation included, is ultimately a self-formation. No one can replace us in the responsible freedom that we have as individuals. ...Future priests should therefore cultivate a series of human qualities, not only out of proper and due growth and realization of the self, but also with a view to the ministry.

For the priests in this study, human development, positive relationships with others, and a sense of service are inextricably connected; they are inseparable.

■

We began by noting the paradox that survey after survey shows that American priests' morale remains high despite the many frustrations, challenges, and pressures they face. We make no claim that the group of priests in this study is a representative sampling of American priests. In fact, we specifically looked for a group of middle-aged priests who impressed others as being particularly effective and full of life.

But we suspect that these priests differ from most other priests more in degree than in kind, because it is likely that most priests who are happy in their priesthood draw life in the same way as our sample. We suspect too that other priests, at least in their reflective moments, recognize the ultimate source of that life — that underlying their lives as priests is the Mystery of God present and active. That is gift. That is grace.

In *The Diary of a Country Priest*, the dying priest whispers his last words into the ear of his friend. "Grace is everywhere....!" The priests in this study witness to that same Mystery. Grace is everywhere! Even in the pressures!

There are many stories still to be told!